JFK Stern

DEDICATION

My family

CONTENTS

ACKNOWLEDGMENTS

Miss Allen, and Mrs Smith, Vincent, Georgina, Julius, Lucas, Bilal, Gotz & Gotz, and everyone else, and you know who you are. I am truly grateful for all your help in creating this book. I am lucky to know so many people on whose shoulders I have been able to stand, who are so very much smarter than I and yet were so willing to share their knowledge, experiences and wisdom. Without all of you, and your input, this book would never have been created. Thank you.

1 WHY GRATITUDE?

"If you only say one prayer in the day, make it thank you".
Rumi

Why should I be grateful?

Have you ever asked yourself that?

Come on be honest; it's just you and me here. Quick, nod your head up and down for yes.

Were you told as a child to say thank you and please that it became just another bunch of words you used at the end or beginning of a sentence to get something you wanted? (Did I see you nod your head up and down saying yes?)

Do you ever feel like why do I have to be grateful or what is there to be thankful for as you looked at your life?

Are you fed up of people telling you to "just be grateful" so you started saying thank you when you felt like it or remembered, but it didn't make a difference?

Do you look at your life and only see only the negative but can quite easily look at the life of others and see all the positives? (Have you just nodded yes again? have you been nodding your head the whole way through, affirming all my suspicions about you?), hah, now you made me laugh. Now that we are friends I feel I can ask you some more questions, is that ok? I know you just nodded and said yes because that's what friends do, right?. Thanks. Ok, let us continue.

Perhaps you were always told to count your blessings, and you got fed up of being told that because you couldn't see any in your life and didn't understand as a child what that meant and were too scared to ask. Maybe you still feel like that and are too frightened or just uncomfortable, talking about it.

Maybe you have felt or feel at present there is nothing to be grateful for and feel you are just an average human being. You find yourself

3

struggling to make ends meet, living from pay cheque to pay cheque each month. Meanwhile, other people have more than you do. They have a more beautiful house, a more excellent car, a better job, eat out, go on exotic holidays several times a year, have savings to fall back on. Besides, they have what you desperately need, i.e. good credit so they can borrow and never seem to go without, while your life is barely hanging on by a thread. You are lucky if you make it to the end of the month.

Is any of this ringing true for you?, or is it that whilst you are reading that although it makes sense you don't feel it applies to you?. Do you just simply feel like you are stuck and in a rut and you just don't know why?.

Perhaps there is a little resentment towards others because they have so much more than you. You feel justified in your resentment towards others because they didn't struggle compared to you. They seem happy while you are still struggling to make ends meet. Does what you have seem infinitesimally small or little compared to what others have? Do you think they don't deserve it and you do?. do you judge others and gossip about their choices, meanwhile desiring what they have?

You may feel angry because you are in a situation not of your liking. Do you struggle to see others come by things you want or think would help to make your life easier?. Maybe you feel other people do not deserve all the stuff because they don't care or value them half as much as you would if you lived their life. Perhaps you feel you would be far far far more grateful if you had everything they have. Maybe you think that those who do have everything you want are not grateful because they came by their wealth so quickly, basically handed to them, for example, a friend who acquired a large sum of money or someone inherited an expensive property or received a gift.

Ok, let's stop for a minute. Do you have a pen and a highlighter pen close to you?. If so grab them, and if not find some. It doesn't matter if the highlighter is blue, yellow or purple. If you can't see one or do not have one, do you have a coloured pencil?. If you don't have either a coloured pencil or a highlighter, then grab a pencil and let us sit down again. Ok, ready, with a pen and highlighter or coloured pencil or pencil in hand, reread the above questions and highlight words and sentences that you feel ring true for you and you can connect with.

Now use the space below to say what you understand or know about gratitude?. How do you feel when someone says "you should be grateful"? or "there is a silver lining in every cloud"?. How does it feel being told that especially if you are not where you want to be in your life right now, and struggling?. What does it feel like when others have more than you?. Who it is in particular that you look at think I could wish I had what they had?.

The replies to the questions are just for you; no one else needs to see it. Please take a moment, as it may not be easy, or it may not necessarily be the first answer that comes to you immediately. So take a moment. I can wait, and when you are ready, we can then proceed.

Please don't skip this part. Remember this is for you unless you choose to share it with someone, so go ahead give it a try, I will wait.

What do you understand or know about gratitude?

....

....

....

....

....

How do you feel when someone says "you should be grateful" or "there is a silver lining in every cloud"?. What does it feel like being told to be grateful especially if you are not where you want to be in your life right now, and struggling?

....

....

....

....

....

....

....

....

How do you feel when others have more than you?

....

....

....

....

....

....

....

....

....

Who is it specifically that you look at and think I wish I had what they have?

....

....

Ok so you did it, well done. It is incredible how thoughts whirring round in your head once written down on paper become so much clearer. Also, you may surprise yourself merely by writing down what you feel. Often we disregard our feelings as we are told its wrong to feel this way or that way, so we bury our emotions. It may be that you discover what you perceived to be true, was not true. Those may not at all be the reasons as to why you thought you felt ungrateful.

It may seem like your best friend is always blessed and never has to think before buying something. You, on the other hand, are still uhming and aaahing, cutting coupons, buy supermarket brands to save money, don't treat yourself, but will spoil others. You are continuously cutting back to make ends meet. You may find that your lack of gratitude has nothing to do with your friend or even the fact she can afford things and you cannot. Maybe just maybe it is more than that. Have you still got your pencil/pen?. If not grab it and write down why deep down you don't feel grateful?. Again you may think you don't know and start beating yourself, so stop right there, there is no need to do that.

Take a moment, sit back and relax into your chair or sofa or wherever you are right now. Be comfortable, and once you are, ask yourself "why am I not grateful"?. Write down the answer or answers below. Perhaps you are grateful but don't honestly truly feel thankful because you think it is not enough, maybe you want more or bigger or better to feel grateful honestly. Write down whatever comes up for you. It is not about good or bad. It is crucial that we get to see what gratitude looks like for you. You will get to see the why? and What?.

Moreover, the where?. In your life, are you held back? Maybe it is not holding you back, and you are the attitude of gratitude personified and feel you merely require a little tweaking. Where ever you right now is fine. Take your time, and I am here for you. We are on this journey together.

Why are you not grateful? (Be specific and detailed and write down everything. All the reasons you think and feel that make up for you not being grateful). Don't worry, like most people who write this list, yours too will be very long. So write as much as you need to in the area below.

....

....

Gratitude

....

....

....

....

....

....

....

....

....

....

....

....

....

....

....

....

....

....

....

....

....

....

....

....

....

Many of us have never really understood what gratitude is and believe it is very much about saying "thank you". Others have had so many struggles in life that they don't see where there is anything to be grateful. That may be the case for someone born into wealth whereby all their needs and wants are taken care of that they feel empty inside. They too don't feel they have anything good in their life to be grateful.

Do you associate having lots of things with the being grateful? Write your answer in the brackets. Yes or No (.............)

Do you think that everyone who has amassed great wealth is grateful? Write your answer in the brackets Yes or No (.............)

Do you think it is the grateful people who are happy or happy people who are grateful? Write your answer in the space below

....

Maybe you hated being poor and as a child was made fun of at school. As a result, you may now feel that everything you earned is all because of your hard work, skills and talent. It almost broke you, working all that overtime to get to where you are now, so why do you have to be grateful?. You feel it was you and you alone who got you to where you are now. It was because of your perseverance, sheer will-power and grit determination that you got to where you got to. You don't see why, or who to be grateful to and your determined not to be thankful.

Ok so let us continue.........

There is much research that has been done to show the sheer benefits of gratitude on health and wellbeing. These include the works of Robert Emmons, professor of psychology at UC Davis. Robert is the author of several books on gratitude including "Why Gratitude is Good". David Steindl-Rast is a Benedictine monk who frequently talks about appreciation. David states that it is grateful people who are happier. Moreover, it is gratitude that leads to happiness and not happiness that makes people grateful.

In comparison, Steve Harvey, comedian and TV show host made a profound statement when discussing gratitude. He said "if you are not thankful, if you are not grateful for what you have, why would God give you more stuff for you to then not to be grateful, thankful and appreciative?. Why would he do that? It does not make any sense; it goes against him....... it goes against everything that makes sense .... the lack of gratitude is one of the biggest blessing blockers that there is. Why would God give you more stuff for you not to be grateful for? have you ever looked at it that way?". Harvey goes on to say "maybe you don't have any more than you have because you are not thankful and appreciative for what you have had".

I don't know about you, but that gave me the chills the first time I listened to it. Something could be said so many times, and it is just background noise until one day you hear the same thing said differently and it suddenly makes sense. I found Harvey's words resonated with me and made sense particularly, as he openly admitted to struggling with the very idea of gratitude and how it took him years to understand it. He then went on during the show to joke with his audience that he hoped it would not take them as long to "really get it".

Meanwhile, American politician, Frank A Clark cuts to the chase with his straight talking " if a fellow isn't thankful for what he's got, he isn't likely to be thankful for what he's going to get".

Oprah Winfrey, a philanthropist, actress, TV show host and billionaire who has interviewed hundreds of famous personalities, beautifully highlights her own life experience when she said "be thankful for what you have; you'll end up having more. If you concentrate on what you don't have, you will never, ever have enough". Miss O has often spoken about her upbringing, and the sheer gratitude she feels for all that life has given her. Oprah's life was one of poverty and abuse. The highest hopes for her by her grandmother were to be a maid.

Oprah Winfrey, Frank A Clark and Steve Harvey are all echoing in their own words from their personal experiences and the journey of life what Greek philosopher, Epictetus said, which was, "he is a wise man who does not grieve for the things which he has not, but rejoices for those which he has"

Take a moment to pause and reflect on what all these different personalities are saying, before rushing off and reading the next sentence because inevitably as the old saying goes, unless you are grateful for what you already have in life, how will you ever be grateful when you have or get more?. Maybe you are only thankful when you get what you want and the way you want it. Even then, you grow unhappy after you see a newer, better or shinier version of the same thing.

How can anything new come into your life when you are not even aware of all that you have?. It may be something so great and yet so simple as being on this side of the grass and still breathing.

In the space below write down your understanding of gratitude. What does the word mean for you?. What kind of thoughts and feelings come up when you hear the phrase gratitude? Be honest, because this is for and about you. Even if you feel that it does not bring up positive feelings, write those down. If positive feelings and thoughts come up for you hearing the word gratitude write them down. Don't just write thankfulness, or grateful. Think what the word means for you. What do you associate the word with?, Do you like gratitude as a word? Do you like the images and mental chatter the word raises in your head as you think about it?. Is it a concept for you?. What does it mean to you?, Does it mean anything apart from what others have said it means?

Write down exactly how you feel about the word, no holding back, ok. (Say yes, loudly so I can hear you)

....

....

....

....

....

....

....

....

....

....

....

Do you remember the first time someone told you to be grateful, and you didn't want to be? (write down the name of the person)

....

....

Okay, now write down what happened as a result of not wanting to be grateful. Write down everything you remember about the incident. Everything, you remember. Where were you? The day? , the year? the location?

....

....

....

Gratitude

....

....

....

....

....

....

....

....

....

....

....

....

....

....

....

....

....

....

It was utterly fascinating undertaking research for this book. So many people shared their understanding of what gratitude was for them. They also shared if it meant anything to them. The common theme throughout was that everyone had questions about the topic. So I have incorporated them into the various chapters.

2 WHY IT HAS EVERYTHING TO DO WITH YOU

"Gratitude is more of a compliment to yourself than someone else"
Raheel Farooq

Does it matter if I say thank you?.............(write yes or no)

What's the big deal anyhow?.................. (yes or no)

Do you ever tell yourself that no one else is grateful or expresses it to you; so why should I?............... (yes or no)

Do you think it is over-rated?................... (yes or no)

Have you ever been called ungrateful?.................. (yes or no)

Do you call others ungrateful?................ (yes or no)

Do you feel no one has a right to tell you to be grateful, I mean look how little you have compared to others?

.... (yes or no)

Do you feel gratitude is just an airy idea, and as long as you say "thank you", it doesn't matter?.................... (yes or no)

Do you feel that you have got this far in life without being grateful, so why start now?..................... (yes or no)

Alternatively, do you think you have everything because of your efforts and created it yourself if anything people should be grateful to you?...................... (yes or no)

Do you say "thank you" because it is unbecoming not to; you don't want people thinking you are ungrateful or arrogant? .... (yes or no)

Do you do things, or give to others, so they are grateful to you, however, have a hard time accepting help or things yourself?........... (yes or no)

Do you feel God owes you?.......... (yes or no)

Do you feel people owe you?............. (yes or no)

Who is it that you feel should be grateful to you

....

Why do you think they should be thankful to you?

....

....

....

Have you ever told them that they are ungrateful and should be grateful?................... (yes or no)

Why didn't you tell them?...

When do you intend to tell them?...

Is there someone to whom you owe gratitude to, but not fully expressed how grateful you are. Who is that?.........
You may have said an obligatory "thanks" in passing at the time. When? (write the date) ....

Do you think you give and it is others who are ungrateful and not giving out of gratitude?................ (yes or no)

You don't believe in anything, follow a particular faith, or believe there is a higher power but don't know anything about it so don't express your gratitude to a power higher than yourself, outside of yourself. If so when was the last time you earnestly expressed your appreciation to your parents?.....................................

Many of us take our parents for granted and buy a gift on mother's or father's day. Others haven't spoken to their parents for years. Often because of something that was said by a parent or because something happened and you interpreted it to mean something as a child. As a result you are still thinking and feeling the same emotions that you did as a child; however, now you are no longer a child but always carry those emotions of abandonment, resentment, or loneliness with you. You would rather be right. You don't see why or what to be grateful for in your parents?. Does that sound like what you feel?...................... (yes or no)

The major religions in the world (Islam, Christianity Judaism, Buddhism, Sikhism, Hinduism, Zoroastrianism amongst others) have spoken about the virtues of gratitude for centuries. Poets and Philosophers have also talked about the benefits of being grateful and most importantly expressing gratitude. Greek philosopher, Epicurus said "do not spoil what you have by desiring what you have not; remember what you now have was once among the things you only hoped for". Greek philosopher, Aesop said, "gratitude turns what we have into enough".

One of the many benefits associated with practising daily gratitude frequently mentioned, is that of, improved health and wellbeing. Often keeping a gratitude journal has been recommended. Many well-known personalities have confessed to having some form of daily gratitude habit which they have cultivated over the years. These days you can even buy gratitude jars, where you write down what you are grateful for and pop it into the jar. Another option is listing what you are for grateful in an app on your phone. Later on, we will discuss practical yet straightforward gratitude ideas which can be implemented to compliment your lifestyle.

Tony Robbins a philanthropist and transformational speaker, said to have helped thousands of people around the world in his seminars, including celebrities and politicians. Tony has spoken in interviews about his morning routine whereby he immerses himself in several minutes of gratitude each morning, followed by meditation and jumping into an ice cold pool of water. Oprah Winfrey upon discussing gratitude passionately talks about having kept a gratitude journal for many years. She encouraged her audience to do so, by highlighting the benefits in her own life, particularly in her career. Would you argue when a multi-billionaire is giving you advise?.

Research and advocates of gratitude journals agree that it is better to write things down. There is power in the written word. Many say that you should aim to write down, at least 3-5 things that you are grateful for each day.

The Benefits of practising gratitude include not only improved health and wellbeing but better social interactions. Gratitude, when put into action, creates a powerful social impact by strengthening our relationships with others. You probably knew this instinctively. It is now evidenced with by science, i.e. what religion and philosophers have been saying for centuries.

We all love feeling and hearing appreciation. It not only makes us feel good as the giver, but it also makes the receiver feel good. It is the acknowledgement of the good provided combined with the appreciation that has a powerful impact. Recognition shows us that what we did was recognised by the other person without us having to explain it to them. Saying "thank you" and showing appreciation to one another has been shown by researchers to strengthen relationships. I know, I know, your thinking everyone knows this. It is obvious. You say "thank you" and show appreciation, and in return, the other person will do the same by reciprocating. Maybe your thinking I do that already and convinced everyone else does that too. You may be surprised. You can hear all the cynics cheering with "Yes, Yes that is so true. See we were right. What's the point?". I know, not everyone says "thank you" or is genuinely grateful. As a result, rather than upset someone, say nothing they cannot help but express their lack of gratitude out of force of habit. Many religions, philosophers, authors, coaches, point to this lack of authenticity.

During my research for this book, I asked as many people as I could about gratitude. I am so grateful because so many people have directly and indirectly contributed to this book as a result. Initially, it appeared that no one practised gratitude amongst the first few people. I, therefore, continued, wanting a more significant comparison. It became evident that most people did not actively practice gratitude. Some people were aware due to their religion. However, in my small personal study of people no one undertook it daily or understood it, anything other than an excellent idea.

Ok, let's break this down, without sounding like I am about break into a bad rap song. Better still bohemian rhapsody (that was funny admit it, I heard you laugh) Ok now that we have my bad jokes sorted and out of the way; what I was trying to say before you distracted me was how not everyone does say thank you or is grateful. Ok, I hear you, you want me to give you an example. Glad you asked, as I was hoping you would.

So far I have kept quiet about myself because I didn't want you to feel this wasn't about you. However, now that we are getting closer, get on, and are friends, I think I can tell you more and be more open with you, don't you agree? (quick nod your head). Instead of studying for one of my exams one day I spent all afternoon searching for a present for a friend. She really wanted the newly publicised mascara on the market that made your eyelashes look thick and lusciously long, voluptuous with extra strength and full of volume (never knew mascara could do so much, and all at the same time. In comparison, I struggle on a daily basis to multi-task typing and trying to eat my breakfast). This mascara, although advertised on the TV, which is where she had fallen for it, wasn't necessarily available in the majority of high street stores. I was determined to buy it for her. So off I went, leaving behind my studying, going from one store to another, and I kid you not when I tell you that I spent hours walking until my legs hurt and ankles swelled, the likes of which even elephants have not seen. (No it is not because I am ancient. I know you are probably now thinking that imagining me walking in the city where the streets have no name). I felt that the major stores like Boots or Selfridges or Debenhams, John Lewis, Fenwicks or Harrods would have this all great mascara that enabled a woman to transform from tired to bright eyed and bushy tailed every morning. (Those of you who are probably shouting at the book, yes I am aware, there is man makeup. Men do use make-up, so, if you do insert the word 'man' after the word 'enabled' we have satisfied both parties and its equal in the world of equality. As a result, it should read 'that enabled a man to transform from tired to bright eyed and bushy tailed every morning. Alternatively, how about we do away with the woman and man and just put human or person?).

None of the stores had the mascara for humans in stock (oops, I almost typed human mascara. Can you imagine the amount of attention this book would have received if I had?. Rest assured no humans beings underwent any painful procedures during the making of this book.) Oxford Street, Regent Street and Leicester Square and

Trafalgar Square all had the same stores. I kept trying each one, thinking maybe the next one had it in stock.

If I had counted all the miles I had walked I would have reached Mount Everest twice over. I am absolutely sure I would have. (Stop laughing. My legs and feet were telling me, and they never lie. I am genuinely surprised I didn't call an ambulance. I would have been asking for a tank of oxygen first to recover. Followed up by gallons of laughing gas to laugh at the absurdity of the whole situation, I had created. I was too tired to even feign a laugh. It really would have been nice to be picked up and placed on a stretcher for a rest, and then driven home as a priority with the blue light and sirens blaring forcing buses, taxis and cars to move because shopping for a mascara had taken its toll. It was just too much. New levels to aspire to for those of you who like buying mascara, or love shopping).

The next morning when I gave my friend the new shiny present; guess what happened?..... Well, I don't know about you, but I was expecting a big smile, expressions of total glee after receiving a much sought after present., and yes a big thank you upon being opened. Instead, a half-hearted thank-you was muttered and an unimpressed look. Wow. Not the reaction I was expecting if I am honest with you. Firstly it was a pretty expensive gift — it had not long since been on the market which I had tried my very best to get. Secondly, I spent my whole afternoon running around to find the gift. There was no acknowledgement of any of this or even an expression of appreciation of a gift. A gift that wasn't available everywhere because it was so new to the market that not all the stores stocked it yet.

I think Simon Sinek, the author of 'Why' explains this concept beautifully in an interview. He spoke about a particular incident on a plane. He sat next to someone who was not very considerate. It led him to feel uncomfortable. He explains during the interview, that normally he would offer to take down a fellow passengers suitcase down at the end of the journey. However, on this occasion, he did not offer that act of generosity. It was due to the way his fellow passenger behaved. Simon mentions he had a choice and could have taken it down out of superiority and made a comment. He chose not to do that. Instead, he walked away from the situation and his fellow passenger. If you get a moment, do watch Simon's YouTube video. It is funny, probably because it is true, and we have all have been in a similar situation. Simon's story highlights how we are unlikely to give again or reciprocate when someone does not extend their appreciation or acknowledge us.

The story I mentioned above is one example of a lack of gratitude. I don't know about you, but I struggle, yes I do. When you give, and people don't reciprocate by way of merely acknowledging your giving and saying thank you.

Although they are only two words, they are heavy on the scales. These two simple words when spoken with sincerity will mean that people will more than likely help you again or give you another gift. It leaves both parties feeling good, i.e. the giver and the receiver. Many philanthropists and highly successful people who give generously, often describe a feeling similar to a runner's high. They say it is like a glow. Both the giver and the receiver benefit through the combination of sharing and appreciation, as they give out of the recognition for all they have. As a result, many donate their wealth and time to those who are less fortunate than they are.

I heard an amusing anecdote from a leader in a seminar regarding a village in India. Everyone wanted Gandhi's spirit to continue, but no one wanted to do the work, they all pointed to those in the next town. Similarly we want to receive rather give. Once Gandhi himself on a train journey lost a shoe. He therefore, took off the other shoe and casted it in the direction of the one that he had lost. People asked him why he did that. He explained that one shoe when found by someone would be of no use to him. Is it not better that he has a matching pair to put to good use?

Whom would you prefer to give a present to from the following two examples?. The person who is grateful, saying thank you, beaming with appreciation and hugs you to show you that they appreciate what you gave them or did for them. Your sure that if you gave this person a painted rock, they would still smile, thank you and be grateful.

Alternatively, would you prefer to give a present to the person whom you know will say " oh you shouldn't have" and then continues to whine "oh it's too small"? "It's not my colour". "Do you have the receipt because I might be able to change it for something better, that suits me better?". "Maybe Ross will like it, why don't you give it to him instead?". "It's kind of you, but I don't like these kinds of things". "oh you shouldn't have bothered". At no point does the person express their gratitude and thank you for thinking of them and buying them a gift. Instead, all you hear is the criticism of what you brought them. I am sure like many people you wouldn't feel encouraged or enthused about buying this person another gift, and you are therefore unlikely to do so as you recall how unappreciative they were of the last gift you gave them.

No one likes their efforts to go unnoticed, and no one wants to feel unappreciated. We know this instinctively and don't like it when people do it to us, but often we will do it to others because we are busy, under pressure, feel stressed, worried about many things and forget to acknowledge and be grateful of the good that we do have and receive.

As I reflected on what had happened I tried to think about how my friend felt and why she was not grateful I realised this whole thing wasn't about her, it was about me. I expected a thank you. I understood I had given with the expectation of receiving rather than giving because I wanted to give and give out of joy because I was already grateful for what I had and could honestly say that I giveth because as the old saying goes "my cup runneth over". Instead, I was not feeling grateful but resentment and resignation because I had given away what I didn't have and needed myself and yet was giving it away to others. I was blaming others that they weren't giving to me and then expecting gratitude in return.

Have you ever done something similar, whereby you have given to others and expected them to give in return?. A great example comes from John Gray in his wonderfully helpful book 'Men are from Mars and Women Are From Venus'. Gray clarifies how instead of expecting your partner to take care of all your needs you need to take care of your own needs so in essence, you can give because your cup is full. Gray highlights that issues occur in a relationship when we give away the very thing we may have or don't have ourselves. We expect others to replenish our empty cups.

Where do you find yourself giving away what you don't have? (write down a specific area and then provide specific details in that area. Write down the people involved, what you give away? Why do you give in that way? How often you give it away? Do you feel guilty if you don't give in that way? Have you always given from this one specific area?, When did you start giving in this particular way? How does it impact you? How does this giving impact others?).

It may be that you find yourself giving all your time away to everyone at work that you have very little time for family life. You may be so busy doing everything else for everyone else that you have little or no time to take care of yourself. The only time you do is when you become ill and are forced to rest and recuperate. You give away the most valuable resource away at the detriment of your health and wellbeing. You may do this so naturally that it occurs as second nature. However, you feel burdened and become resentful of the very people you are giving. It may be your job colleagues, your friends or your family. You may be giving away money when you need it yourself. It can be any number of things. Pick one area of your life where you struggle the most and write about that one in detail. You may want to write free flow with whatever comes up for you. You may be clear on exactly what that is and how you feel. If you need some help, use the questions listed above to help you.

....

....

Gratitude

....

....

....

....

....

....

....

....

....

....

....

....

....

....

....

....

....

....

....

....

....

....

....

....

....

....

Where do you find yourself feeling resentment and resignation? In this area, you feel no gratitude, and you notice nothing is changing. You have tried so many times to transform that area of your life, but nothing works. (be as specific as you can be, this is just between you and me. So be as honest as is possible. If you want to share it with someone ok but right now focus on just writing it as it is)

....

....

....

Gratitude

....

....

....

....

....

....

....

....

....

....

....

....

....

....

....

3 GRATITUDE IS LIKE BEING TOLD TO EAT YOUR VEGGIES

"Do not spoil what you have by desiring what you have not"
Epicurus

Gratitude is a bit like being told to eat more fruit and vegetables. We all know that we should be more grateful and appreciative on a day to day basis for what we. However, we struggle with putting it into practice and can't seem to be grateful. Many of us get uncomfortable when reminded. Even when we know, it is for our good. We feel that if we are thankful, then we won't strive so much because we will end up being satisfied with what we have, which we are not. So it is better not to think about gratefulness and continue to push forward in a world that is all about targets and performance and remain driven for success. We strive to be successful in our lives as an employer, an employee, as a father, as a mother, as a student, as a friend, as a husband, as a wife, in our jobs, at home, in relationships, in communities, in mosques, in churches, in the synagogues and as nations. You may feel like after all that striving do I have to be now grateful for the way things are, with what is, which is what everyone appears to be saying to you. You might not be happy with the state you live in, day in day out it is the same. You want better a better life with; better health, more money, a bigger house, a second home abroad, well-behaved children, a better car, better relationships, be those family, marital, friends or romantic.

Alternatively, you want a better life with the best of everything rather than any one thing. The advocates of gratitude appear to be saying that, rather than focusing on everything that you don't have and keep complaining about to everyone who will listen, focus on what you do have. Do you complain so much about what you don't have, that even you are tired of hearing yourself? (admit it, have you ever done that to yourself?. Did I see you nod your head?; are you still nodding your head?. Remember we are friends now, you can tell me anything). Focus on what you do have. Instead of focusing on the ear infection or toothache, or cough, focus on being grateful you don't have a severe or significant illness, be thankful that it is possible to treat it. It is not bronchitis or you don't have to have all your teeth pulled out or you at least your eardrum is not perforated. It is more about the good that you do have rather than the problem you do have. It is a case of perspective. Where do you focus?. Are you someone who always focuses on the lack or are you someone who can look at a situation and see the good in it.

There is an old story about a pair of twin boys whom the parents were worried about, so they took them to a psychologist. The parents informed the psychologist how one son was unhappy all the time regardless of what they gave him. He never seemed happy with anything compared to his twin brother. The psychologist separated the boys and placed them in two separate rooms. One boy put in a room filled with muck while the other boy went into a different room full of muck. After a while both parents and the psychologist looked in on the boys and the one who was always sad, always complaining, sat huddled in the corner complaining to himself "why is it like this"? "why does this always happen to me"? "where are my the toys" and "why did he have to be here"?. The parents were saddened to see how unhappy their young son was and worried about his future.

The psychologist then moved along with the parents to the second room where their other twin son was. He was throwing the horse manure everywhere and was cover with it. He had a big smile on his face, shouting "where's the pony"? "where is the pony"?. "There has to be a pony here somewhere, with all this horse manure" all the while laughing and enjoying himself. "The boy knew where there was so much manure there had to be a pony.

The moral of the story being, yes you guessed it, making the most of where you are. You will hopefully reach where you want to get to, but you have to appreciate what you already have. Put another way as quoted by motivational speaker Zig Ziglar "gratitude is the healthiest of all human emotions. The more you express gratitude for what you have, the more likely you have even more to express gratitude for".

If I am honest with you, this old story didn't mean much to me except it was a good story until I read and heard the author of 'Chicken Soup for the Soul', Jack Canfield. He mentioned his wife telling him about a golden Buddha that had been covered up by monks with mud during the war to avoid soldiers removing it. Jack's wife highlighted to him how people rather like the Buddha had gold beneath all the mud. As they went through life, they collected more and more dirt over the years. They couldn't see all that they had already.

If we are walking around disconnected, covered in mud, and yet are searching for humanity in others for them to share with us, do think that will ever help us to be more grateful?. No?. Right?. How can we be thankful for others when we are not even aware of all that we have. Forget all the material stuff you have, your family, friends, the roof over your head, your wife, husband, children, pets, forget everything. Now when was the last time you woke up, breathed, opened your eyes and said thanks as a result of sheer appreciation for being alive?.

Seriously, don't just rush onto the next sentence. Take a moment, make a note on the side of this page, when was the last time you woke up grateful for just being given another day to live?. Don't go silent and grumble, or dismiss the question. Maybe you are feeling proud of yourself because you are enlightened and said "thank you" when you woke up this morning. So to you, I ask how deep was your appreciation?; was it a routine you undertake because you heard it is good to be grateful so you say it and get it over and done with then take a shower and brush your teeth?. Alternatively, do you feel the feelings and depth, so they are not just words that you say but feel them on a deeper level?. If you get off track during the day, are you able to bring yourself back to that place of gratitude with personal appreciation and in a sense recalibrate yourself?

I am not saying it is easy because the minute you wake up it may feel like a battle with your brain and it may be that you didn't feel like waking up and would rather lay back down and sleep some more. Within seconds of waking up, you start worrying and focus on what is complete and all the things that require completion. It is not the Matrix where Samuel L. Jackson pops out with his cool sunglasses and asks you which pill you want and because you are the chosen one; it just happens. It takes work on your part to build a new muscle. There is no magic pill, plus pill popping is overrated. Trust me you will be grateful when you have developed your new gratitude muscle. I cannot wait for you to write to me and tell me. Deal? (nod your head and say, yes. Say yes louder because I didn't hear it. I don't care if you look crazy and what will people say. Say Yes, go on .... say it, louder. See it feels good doesn't it?)

Okay, let's go back to the golden Buddha covered in mud. In essence, Jack's wife's story provides us with a better understanding of the twin boys., one twin was continually asking and wanting for more and miserable at the same time. In comparison, the second twin was having fun with what he had, i.e. horse manure and was full of gratitude, appreciation, excitement and anticipation of finding the pony who had produced all the manure. You may have noticed how the first twin was stuck in his thinking, living in the past. Living in the past of toys and being given everything. He did not want to participate so sat sulking in the corner of the room. He could hear the squeals of laughter and joy from his brother in the other room.

Instead of creating possibilities within the current situation he decided to live in the past. As a result, he declined to participate in his own life. He could have opened the door and gone and joined his brother in fun. He could have walked out of the room and looked for his parents. However, he chose to be defeated by his circumstances and wanted to be rescued and taken back to the security of his home with his toys. As a result, he wasted his time, missed an opportunity, caused distress for those around him and made the circumstances he was in worse.

Many of us can feel like this as adults and feel stuck and unable to move or see anything else apart from the situation as it is. You can imagine his possible future if he does not transform. His twin was a smart kid who was aware of the old saying; "where there's muck, there's brass". In his case a pony.

"where there's muck, there's brass" was found to be true because a particular water company wrote an article. Their lab boffins confirmed their findings that there was gold within the muck. Okay, if you are sitting there and work in the water industry and wracking your brains (which I know you will be. I bet you will now pretend you are not just because I said it. Right?. Yes, I thought so) thinking it is your company. Well, it may be. So here is the deal. Write in, and you could be in with a chance of a surprise gift. No not a pony. No not gold. No not a trip to California or Japan for a 24-carat gold ice-cream. If you happen to visit either one, do take me with you. I have already packed my bags and a copy of Conde Nast. It is an offer of a free signed copy of this book. It will be my gift to you to gift to someone you love or someone at the water company. "Oh goodness". Look what I have now created. I can hear everyone else who doesn't work in the water industry saying they want a signed copy too. Ok. Ok. Let everyone join in. Take a guess which water company then send your answers. "Phew". Now that we have got that all sorted, shall we carry on before I start offering pedigree ponies as prizes from my back garden?.

4 CONNECTION IN YOUR GRATITUDE

"expressing gratitude is a natural state of being and reminds us that we are all connected"
Valerie Elster

We often forget how our lack of gratitude and appreciation affects others. You may already know how your lack of appreciation has made someone else feel. Someone may have told you how your lack of recognition made them feel. You may have said someone else what you think about their lack of gratitude. Is it possible that the lack of humanity and connection you may be feeling and complaining about in others is a result of your lack of appreciation?.

It is never easy to have a mirror held up to our weaknesses. We are so used to being told what to do, how to be, where to go, and when to do something. As children, we drown those requests and demands out. Then as adults we reignite those child capabilities, i.e. drowning out of peoples voices when told to do something. No one likes to feel they are forced to do something. So we pretend to be grateful to make others happy. While all the time we, are making ourselves unhappy by being inauthentic. We end up being like this with ourselves and others and think we are fooling others and act surprised when they call us out on it. We ask "how did you know"?

Take a moment, pick up that pen and highlighter again, and let's look at a specific time, I am sure there were many and you have so many examples to choose from, but let's pick one for now. Ready .... great, see now that we are clearly friends I know your already nodding your head even before I asked you). Ok, let's start.

Please take a moment, pick up that pen and highlighter again, and let's look at a specific time, I am sure there were many, and you have so many examples to choose from, but let's pick one for now. Ready?. Great. See now that we are friends I know your already nodding your head even before I asked you). Ok, let's start.

....

....

....

....

....

....

....

....

....

....

....

....

....

....

....

....

....

....

....

....

....

....

Now write down how you felt when the person you helped expressed their gratitude to you. Try writing more than it made me happy or I was glad they said "thanks". Look at really describing how helping the other person really made you feel?

....

....

....

....

....

....

....

....

....

....

....

....

....

Did it make you want to help them again and if so why?

....

....

....

....

....

....

....

Did it make you feel more connected to the person and if
so how?

....

....

....

....

....

....

....

....

....

Did it make you feel grateful to know the other person?
Did it make you feel thankful that you had the power to
impact someone's life with so little? Describe how it felt
in detail.

....
....
....
....
....
....
....
....
....

Did it make you appreciate that it doesn't take much and if so will you do it again? If you honestly feel you would not, help or give again then write that down. Also, write why you felt that way. (no one is judging you, even if your judging yourself, this is for you only. When you are ready and if you feel you want to, then share what you wrote but you don't ever have to. So write it as it is)

....
....
....
....

....

....

....

....

....

....

....

....

....

....

....

....

....

....

If you believe in God, did you appreciate God more as a result?. Did you become more grateful for what you have to God?. If you don't believe in a higher power, did you become more thankful for all that you have that enabled you to help someone else? Write down precisely what happened and how you felt. What did it make you realise?. What in particular were you grateful for as a result of giving/helping someone?

....

....

....

....

....

....

....

....

....

....

....

....

....

....

....

....

....

....

5 GRATITUDE ROUTINE

"Cultivate the habit of being grateful for every good thing that comes to you, and to give thanks continuously. And because all things have contributed to your advancement, you should include all things in your gratitude".
Ralph Waldo Emerson

I don't know about you but when someone says the word 'routine' like most people you stop listening. You start to roll your eyes and check out because it sounds like work and boring. There are many routines we undertake on a daily, weekly, monthly and yearly basis. Another way of looking at it is to look at the things you do consistently or out of habit. You may wake up every morning, have breakfast, get dressed and go to the gym before going to work. Perhaps you have a daily routine where you go to your favourite coffee shop and buy a croissant, a muffin, a muesli bar and a cappuccino and walk to work.

You sit at the same desk, in the same chair, use the same mug, eat the same sandwiches for lunch at the same time at the same table in the same place, read the same genre of books or magazines and talk to the same people. Maybe your daily routine is to start your day at work huddled in the kitchen and talk about how bad things are and how awful your colleagues are and how bad the boss is, and you can't understand how she/he ever got the job. How if you had gotten the role you would have been brilliant and the company would make millions of pounds. Everyone would get bonuses every week. Moreover, everyone would listen to you and love you because you would be the world's best boss.

Alternatively, you don't focus on work problems, but instead, your routine is to gossip about family and friends and how bad they are. How you don't get to see the kids enough, or how she/he doesn't let you do what you want. You never have enough money. How he doesn't make you feel alive, wanted, feminine and beautiful enough. How you never go out, or on holidays, or date nights, and meals out because even though you both work you cannot afford it.

Then again, it's the in-laws that are the problem. It's the children fighting constantly and drained as you try to juggle everything and everyone's lives. Soon enough you start talking about how even the cat and dog don't get along and each night they seem to pop out of the cat flap separately, one after the other. The cat first of course.

They pop out for a few hours to take a stroll and get some fresh air. They also pop in to see their other friends in the neighbourhood.

Are you sitting there reading and nodding your head thinking of the people in your life whom you know that do that? (I knew it, I knew it. See we know each other so well now. As your friend, I knew that you would be thinking of all the people you know that do that every morning. Are you smiling? Yes?. See, I caught you out again). Do you realise and acknowledge when you behave like that?. What your daily routines are made up of?. Were you only able to see the habits and routine behaviours of others around you? (I know, I know..... you weren't expecting me to call you out, and trust me I almost didn't, but what kind of friend would I be if I didn't right...... not a very authentic one, that is for sure. Lucky you, I am all about authenticity and integrity, so you get the real deal)

It is not about good or bad. Routines can be helpful because they can serve us. It helps you to take time out and be exercising, eating well, resting and taking care of your inner/emotional/spiritual wellbeing. It's not all about making the next pay cheque, continuously living in survival mode.

56

Are you sitting there getting overwhelmed and feel you can't transform, it's all too late, or you have tried before, and nothing worked?

Do you feel there is nothing for you to learn here? Do you think that your life is ok, it could be worse? Alternatively, do you think that at least you're not like those people at work who are continually gossiping, whining and blaming someone else? It is always the other person's fault.

My daily commute for years has consisted of travelling on a packed train or tube (be sure to say hi, when you see me. ok.) and I noticed how every journey, be it bus, tube, walking, or train, people would always be talking, and it would still be the same conversation. Whoever, was talking would be sharing how it was 'HER' fault, and another group, or couple, or even on the phone (yes loudly for the whole carriage to hear) would be talking about how it was 'HIS' fault. I was genuinely intrigued wondering if this one woman and one man went around causing all these people grief because never in my entire life had I heard 'HER' or 'HIS' so many times. The temptation was there so many times to say something. I have wanted to say to the group/couple/person on the phone who is not being subtle in their conversation "you might want to talk to the person rather than about them". Other times I am tempted to point out that perhaps they should be grateful because the other person is highlighting parts of their character and way of being which makes uncomfortable. You might be feeling oh my goodness I thought this book was about gratitude and may feel like why are we talking about you now, and it's becoming all a bit too personal (are you shaking your head in agreement? Well okay if you are and good if you are not).

This whole book is personal and was and will be from beginning to end. It's all about you connecting with gratitude, and as you read through you will notice a golden thread; we are all the same. Yes, I know, amazing isn't it?. There was you thinking we are all separate and you were all on your own, special and unique (don't get me wrong, and I don't want to undo what your mamma told you. You are, special and unique, you are, but your also the same as everyone else.

Let us bring this closer to home by me sharing a story with you. Ready?, sitting comfortably?, (I feel like I am about to read little red riding hood – stop laughing... I am way too young to be sitting with a red tartan blanket over my lap, left leg over the right leg and a comfy woolly warm slipper dangling off the left foot with the other firmly on the ground. Round silver framed glass spectacles lowered to the bridge of my nose looking down ready to read. Sitting in my rocking chair in front of an open roaring red/orange, pine log fire). Gosh, the things I have to go through all in the name of artistry; no one tells you about this stuff at school, do they?. Come to think of it no one does at college or university either. Answers on a postcard to JFK Stern, PO Box 2874517, England regarding what they should teach at school/college/university"? (that's a made-up address in case some of you funnies out there start writing to tell me what they should be teaching). Okay, that is enough banter and horsing around for one day.

Now that you are seated comfortably let us get back to the story itself before this becomes a book about sending me postcards and horsing around.

Sometimes you can meet someone and think they have no right to complain because they have everything They have the money, the house, the family, the extended family, the homes, the 4 holidays a year, the private plane, the yacht, a wealthy partner, the perfect kids with the best private education money can buy, eat out at least 4 times a week. They invited to all the right parties that you and I could not attend if we paid for them (well ok, maybe you could. When you do go, please send me an invite so I can be your plus one. I must warn you though, that you may be sorry when we get there, and you see how many times I eat from those silver platters as the waiters walk around with oeuvres. Sometimes that is all they serve and don't tell you. You then have to stand around for aeons for the auction to start for one of their charity events. By this time you would happily bid £2000 for a piece of bread and some soup. I may well end up being your plus two by the end of the evening).

Lo and behold to your surprise all you ever hear them do is complain and gossip about other people. I was talking to someone recently who by any scope of the imagination was wealthy. It was not necessary for this individual to work. As a result, you would assume that they would be grateful. Not once did I hear this woman express any appreciation for the apartment in Knightsbridge, for the private chef that she and her husband hired who would make whatever they wanted at whatever hour. Don't get me wrong I am sure the chef's paid well. However, it was the sheer lack of gratitude that surprised me. The lack of appreciation continued towards having a nanny who took care of their children. The lack of recognition continued into every area of this woman's life from having to work, not paid enough (although she commanded an excellent salary), her parents, her siblings, her children, her mother, her previous work colleagues, her current work colleagues and workplace.

I know, I know, I can already imagine what you're thinking. If you had all that, you would be thanking you're lucky stars every day. Really?. Really?. Are you so sure, because everyone says that?. Everyone says how they would be so different. I recently heard a motivational speaker, Tony Robbins talking on one of his YouTube videos where the discussion was around transformation, and the question about money popped up. Tony (sounds like I know him, maybe I should refer to him as Mr Robbins, but that seems so formal, what to do...... you never know once he reads this, and we meet maybe I can call him Robbs for short. It would thereby totally cut out the need to call him Tony or by his surname) stated that more money has, in essence, nothing to do with it and that if you were a jerk before, having more money would accentuate that, and if you were loving, kind, gracious and giving, having more money would merely accentuate that.

The woman we spoke about earlier is a multi-millionaire several times over if you combine her and her partner's total wealth. Regardless of their wealth and good health and looks, they are unhappy and ungrateful. It can be difficult to imagine how? Moreover, why? Someone with everything cannot see and appreciate what they have. Often it is a blind spot, and it only comes into full view when it's taken away, decreases or causes some issue.

Okay, take a moment and think about yourself and the areas where you have plenty. I didn't just write that story so it would be a good story, the end. No. I could give many more examples, but that is not the point. The point is for us to look at ourselves, like we do when we brush our teeth in the morning, shave, put on makeup. You get to see you and what you look like in the mirror rather than the image you hold of yourself in your head. So take a moment and think of where in your life do you have plenty and then think of the last time you were grateful for that which you have in that area. So write that down below. Be specific what, and why you are thankful and appreciative of that, you have in that area. Focus on what you already have NOT what you don't have and only write that in the space below.

Maybe you don't have a tonne of money, but you have a great supportive family or a group of really great friends that are always there for you. Maybe you don't have your children but have a loving wife/husband, and you are in a great job with an excellent salary, your respected and highly regarded in your industry.

....

....

....

....

....

....

....

....

....

....

....

....

....

....

Now write down the last time you expressed your gratitude out loud, face to face, to your husband, wife, friends, colleagues, children, parents, siblings, grandparents or family. Write the person/s name and date when you did so

....

Isn't it amazing, many of us will find that in general, we don't, or it was aeons ago when we honestly expressed our appreciation out aloud to people?. I don't mean a half asleep, or I cannot be bothered but I know I need to say it, so I will say it, to make you feel good, "thank you". I mean the kind of "thank you" that shows the other person you noticed them, and acknowledge them as you look them in the eye and say that. It may sound funny, but I appreciated it when a colleague who is well connected and has a tonne of friends eyeing for her attention told me she had written down a note in her diary to remind herself to thank me for the gift I had given her. Now I know she is always busy, but the fact that she cared and wanted to acknowledge her gratitude makes her even more remarkable mainly because she is really wealthy and very independent and doesn't need anything or anyone's help.

The job and the people you are complaining about someone else may be begging to have so that they can avoid receiving food tokens, or avoid having to go to the soup kitchen. They would be grateful for your job so they could buy their food to put on the table, pay their mortgage, go on holidays and afford a new uniform for the kids rather than shop at the charity shop or rely on hand me downs, knowing full well the kids will get picked on and made fun of at school.

The 'HER' your complaining about may have a drunken mother at home she cannot cope with, a partner whom she is with because she sees no way out. She wants to pursue her passion, her true calling but remains in a lowly position at work because she has childcare duties and needs to leave work at 3 pm every day. HER only solace is getting away from it by being at work and going to the pub or drinking a bottle of red wine every evening before going to sleep. The 'HIM' your complaining about may be suffering from a long term health condition, has a considerable mortgage he needs to pay off while he is still grieving over what happened to his previous partner and unable to talk about it even though he is in a new relationship. His only solace is in the bottle in front of the TV every evening although he knows it is not the solution at least it helps him forget everything until tomorrow.

Naturally, it is easier to see other people's behaviours and point out their mistakes and how they behave. Sometimes it is hard to see our reactions. It is a bit like when I drove home at night from my friend's house where one of the neighbours in the opposite house has a small black cat. It was dark, and I was reversing out of the drive, and I did not see the cat. No, I did not do a hit and run okay before you start calling me a cat murderer and call the pet police. Hang on a second; I haven't told you which neighbourhood so I am fine; The point is that I couldn't see the cat because of a blind spot. Don't worry the cat saw me as the backlights shone and it moved. The point is the cat is alive, and no animals were used or harmed before, during, or after (possibly?) the writing of this book.

Often we see and point out things in others, but we do the very same things and want people to be kind and gentle with us. We may not be aware or even realise we do the very things we complain about in others. These things we don't recognise we do and don't see for ourselves, in essence, are our blind spots. The view is like that of the blind spot in the car. We can't see it. That is why I didn't know the cat was at the back, i.e. it was a blind spot for me.

Ok so let's have a look at what your routines are, i.e. what you regularly do. Maybe we will see some blind spots hiding in there somewhere, or a cat or two. Sometimes we don't even realise habits that we do or have created and done them. Do you know what I mean? (are you nodding your head again....., yes?.....okay so while nodding your head, grab your pen, highlighter and any other coloured pens you choose).

Please take a moment and think about what you do every morning regularly and write it down. You wake up every morning at 6 am when your alarm goes off and get straight out of bed, take a shower, brush your teeth, have a coffee, black with three sugars, and a piece of toast, grab your bag, and your rucksack with your gym kit and set off to work. Write that down and be specific in detail; if you have coffee with milk and two sugars write coffee with two sugars. Be exact with the detail by sticking to the facts. It is not about making yourself wrong or justifying yourself of why you have three sugars, two or none or why you eat a muffin or leftover pizza for breakfast.

Instead, the alarm goes off at, and you lay there and press the snooze button, 3,4,5 times. Write that. You may stay there thinking about all the things you need to do and start prophesying how awful your day is going to be. You worry about what you should have done yesterday, and because you haven't done it your panicking how you're going to manage. You think of the meeting that afternoon. Besides all that, you have a new report to do which requires several hours of research before you even consider asking for and input from the stakeholders. If that's how you think, feel and react every morning, be honest and write that down in the section below.

No one is judging you. You may be judging yourself right now though as you think about what you don't do. Don't start beating yourself up about what you do and don't do. Take a breath, seriously, stop, take a moment, take a deep breath and take a moment to move or even get a drink, no not that kind, a glass of water will do. It isn't that tough that you need to hit the bottle. I don't want you to make this more than it is and make something out of it that it is not. Ok?. What your writing here is for you. You may not want the best for you, but I do because what I am asking you to do, I do it myself first. See. I have struggled with this as well, I have been there so I get you may not want to do these exercises.

Seriously who does? It is easier to go into a state of numbness and sit watching TV and eat pizza, and then eat leftovers for breakfast. Les Brown (International speaker) has said: "if you want an easy life do what is hard and if you want a hard life do what is easy". Les Brown will tell you himself how he grew up poor, was adopted and how many mistakes he made but did not let that stop him. When being pushed down by a group of older boys, Les kept trying to get up even when the boys pushed him back down. Les would not back down even when being pushed down although he was already lying down on the floor, in the bus. He told the older boys "I am still standing up on the inside"!.

On a side note, you may be aware that Les is a twin. He also talks about make-up. I don't want you thinking and feeling you are alone in all of this or I am making the stories up to make you feel better. Others go through similar or often worse situations. Les Brown's life is full of gratitude despite the poverty, the ridicule and setbacks. He openly shares in many of his videos. Definitely worth a watch if you watch YouTube.

Okay, let's come back to what we were discussing, that is, your morning routine. In the space below write down your morning routine. Focus on the facts which may sound something like..... alarm goes off at 6 am. Got out of bed at 6.15am, shower, brush teeth, drink one black coffee, get dressed, wake the three kids, make their sandwiches.....you get the gist right. You could write it like a list as you may run a tight ship in your house or you are just so used to doing what you do that you can do it with your eyes closed. You may want to write what you do each hour. Write it the way it works best for you. Focus on the detail of that you undergo each morning. If you find your rushing write that. If you see you only drink half a cup of coffee because something always happens to stop you finishing the whole cup write that. If you find yourself yelling at the kids to hurry up, or have to go and pull them out of bed write that detail down. Be specific and stick to the facts.

....

....

....

....

....

....

....

....

....

....

....

....

....

....

....

....

....

....

....

....

Now let's move to the afternoon routine. Do the same as the morning, be specific and focus on the detail. If every afternoon you have a sugar dip around 3-4pm and you find yourself snacking on biscuits, cake or something sweet. Write that. Maybe your afternoon routine is to take a walk after lunch or call a friend and have a good natter about how horrible your work colleagues are or how your children never behave or how you wish your partner would do something nice for you for once or how he/she doesn't understand you. Write all those details below.

....
....
....
....
....
....
....
....
....
....
....
....
....
....
....
....
....

....

....

....

....

....

....

....

....

....

....

....

....

....

....

Now the evening routine. You should be on a roll by now. Maybe your head hurts because it means you have had to think about everything you do automatically. Don't worry if that is how your feeling; keep going. Honestly, it is worth it, don't roll your eyes, suck your teeth or look away to see if I am looking over your shoulder. I may not be your guardian angel, but I want the best for you.

Is not examining oneself all about what authenticity and integrity?. As the Socrates said, "an unexamined life is not worth living". We are in this together now, yes you and me. Don't worry I am not going to start telling you, how "I love you" and "you can do this" and "it is for your good". You will have heard that so many times, and if you are like most of us, you don't believe it and it just washes over you. (I know. I know. You are thinking how does this person know everything I am thinking?. They must have spoken to my mum and my best friend. Do you think it would look silly if I put LOL right now? Honestly, that is what I wanted to write, but it just doesn't seem very book author like or very professional. Okay, let's go for ha, ha, ha, no?. How about a simple smiley face then..... I agree to a smiley face, although very tempted to write LOL ☺)

See we get on so well. You had me distracted for a minute. I bet you were thinking I forgot about the evening routine. Well I didn't. So grab your pen kiddo and get to it. In the same format, write down specific details, no need for lengthy ins and outs filled with reasons and justifications of why you do what you do in any set way. See we get on so well. You had me distracted for a minute. I bet you thought I forgot about the evening routine. Well, I didn't. So grab your pen kiddo and get to it. In the same format, write down specific details, no need for the lengthy ins and outs filled with reasons and justifications of why you do what you do in any set way. Just the facts, getting straight to the point (I really want to say "Am I clear solider?". I should work for the army because those boys and gals sure have some routines. Only thing is I am not sure if that off green matches my eye colour if I am honest with you. Perhaps the navy seals instead. Although the blue uniform would make my eyes sparkle, I am not so keen on being woken up in the middle of the night. They wake you up as a part of the drill to see if you have what it takes to join the team. It is not for me in the middle of the night to be woken up to go jogging or stand in the freezing cold seawater doing water aerobics of sorts, with teeth chattering so loud you are sure you could chop the surrounding woods with them and escape. David Goggins may love that kind of thing and who would argue with him. His regime makes even the average seal look sub-seal. Okay enough about me. Enough entertainment let's focus on your evening routine)

....

....

....

....

....

....

....

....

....

....

....

....

....

....

....

....

....

....

....

....

....

....

....

Now, I will take it you have been honest and written everything that you remember you regularly do daily. If you feel you haven't, you can stop here and go back and do so. If you have written in pen and there is no space to add any more details you can take out a notebook or a blank piece of paper and write down your routines. I cannot iterate enough how important it is to take a moment, sit quietly and do this. How can you criticise others when you cannot even be honest with yourself?

Okay, you are on a roll. You are doing great. Let us keep going. Now that we have looked at your daily routines, can we take it that they make up your weekly and monthly and yearly routines? Of course, these are broken when something unexpected happens, which may force you to change for a short time. A change in the short term may be something like an illness which forces you to rest and take care of your health. Maybe even being ill does not affect your routine because you won't allow yourself to relax and be sick. Don't beat yourself up or start making yourself wrong. We all do that, at times, other times we make others wrong and blame them when things don't go the way we want them.

Many, not everyone, I admit, may change their routine or habits if they suffer a significant setback. A considerable setback, maybe health issues/an incurable condition/long term health condition, a death of a loved one, losing your job/redundancy/being fired, losing your company, fraud, watching your life savings go up in smoke due to bad investments or bad advice. Maybe you got the wool pulled over your eyes by friends and lost all your savings. The list goes on and on.

Is it possible that you haven't changed over the years regardless of a significant setback?. Your routine behaviour may be more subtle than that so that you don't even notice how you are operating at home, at school, at college, at university, at work, with friends, with family, with extended family, at work, at parties, in gatherings and the wider community; in essence amongst other people. Sometimes you may catch yourself and as much as you may not want to you find yourself saying or doing the very things others said to you. It may be your mum, dad, grandma, granddad, uncle, or aunt especially if you lived in a close community or saw them often. You may find that you are unconsciously carrying out the same routines and behaviours you grew up around, regardless of whether you liked them or not.

Ok, is your brain now whirring trying to tell me how wrong I am?. However, part of you feels I am right, and part of you feels like I don't want to read this book because your head hurts from thinking?. Do you think this is hard work?. You want to leave it and start the next chapter or stop reading the book altogether. I am not here to tell you it is easy, but I will say that beating yourself up won't help either. If you are a fan of Will Smith, the actor, the original fresh prince of Bel-Air, and YouTube videos, he eloquently explains this very well. Will (look at me, calling him Will like we are the best of buddies, who knows when he reads this we could be) captures this in a significant way. In one of his YouTube, he states: "why are you beating yourself up?; is it not enough that the world is already doing that daily that you feel you have to add to that?". Now ain't that the truth.

So now that we have looked at what your routines and daily habits are let's look at transforming those for a moment. In the space below write down what you want your morning, afternoon and evening routines should be. Be clear and precise. Please do not write it so that it says I do not want..........Write what you want each one of your routines to be. It is oh so tempting to write a bunch of business phrases that people use. They often make no sense or produce great results. I shall, therefore, refrain from outside the box or blue sky thinking. (stop laughing, I can hear you, but at least I know that you know what I am talking about, right?, Nod your head for yes. Good.)

Morning

....

....

Afternoon

....
....
....
....
....
....
....
....
....
....
....
....
....
....
....
....

Evening

....

....

....

....

....

....

....

....

....

....

....

....

....

....

....

....

....

....

Okay so now you have written what your routines are like and what you want them to be. Is there a noticeable difference? Like most people, there will be areas you want to transform. You may wish to convert the morning routine by looking at how long it takes to get up, get the kids ready without a fuss or make time to go to the gym in the morning.

If you have been playing ball and been filling in all the lines with your answers, I honestly want to stop for a moment and commend you. Well done. Now before you get a big head about it all, lets quickly continue. In the space below write down what you are grateful for each morning, afternoon and evening. Do you want an example? (did you nod your head?, good, because I am giving you a case because I am generous like that). So for example, each morning you may be grateful for the tumble dryer because often the kid's clothes are still damp from hanging on the washing line outdoors. You never acknowledged your husband or wife each morning making you a cup of tea or your breakfast. Maybe your grateful that each morning you can drop off the kids or take a walk with the dog to the park. Look at what you do each day and what others do for you that you have regarded it as a given. You take it all for granted that you have forgotten to appreciate it. Genuinely look at your whole day, breaking it down, should make it easier to some degree. We are all creatures of habit. Often we don't even realise how much of our day runs on autopilot. We don't even discern the good that we receive into our lives. Do you know what I mean?. Yes?. Good.

Morning

....
....
....
....
....
....
....
....
....
....
....
....
....
....

....

....

Afternoon

....

....

....

....

....

....

....

....

....

....

....

....

....

....

....

Evening

....

....

....

....

....

....

....

....

....

....

....

....

....

....

I am grateful for my eyes because I usually work on a laptop all day, combined with frequent use of a Smartphone resulting. It often creates eye strain and poor posture. Remember earlier I was saying how sometimes we appreciate things only after they have started to cause an issue, been taken away, decreased or placed by something less desired.

My morning routine involves coffee, yes, sometimes lots of it, so I am grateful for having a great cup of freshly brewed coffee in the morning. I am talking real coffee, not the instant type (just making sure you know that, so that when our paths cross you know what kind of coffee I like and don't offer me tea.) so I am genuinely grateful and really appreciate my silver Italian coffee machine that makes a great cup of coffee in the morning.

Now my two examples are very different, I mean if I ran out of coffee, I could grab one on the way to work, or I could buy a bag of coffee locally, or make a cup at work. In essence, it would not be a big deal compared to eyesight and the ability to see.

My eyesight is a gift I did nothing to earn it. I was given it, born with it. Regardless of whether you believe in God or not, you know if you were to lose your eyesight, you could make it come back even though we all know that we don't act from that, i.e. knowing that we still are not grateful. Every religion and every modern-day leader knows that truly being grateful is having gratitude for the things given to you have no control over, i.e. your blessings. An example of these includes your eyesight, your hearing, the blood pumped by your heart around the body, your heart, your internal organs. The human body and how it regulates and regenerates itself regularly by shedding and replacing cells. It does all this by itself without any intervention from us. Thank goodness because, I assure you if we had to remember to pump our blood or make our nails and hair grow, or regenerate our cells, none of us would be alive. We continuously forget our keys, to attend meetings, put our clothes on inside out, wear different coloured shoes and walk out the door without even realising.

Moreover, get lost even with the satnav. So we are lucky that it is all self-regulated. I sure am grateful because as the old Chinese proverb says "if you don't use your head, you have to use your legs", and as it is with most of us, we forget things and are constantly going back to go get the thing we forgot. So imagine us doing that with our breathing, heart or digestion a day, week, month or year later. No. I would rather not but am sure grateful that I don't have to manage that along with everything else. Can you imagine the number of notifications on your phone would never be ending? Your life would rely on you remembering to do all of them. It would drive you nuts, and you would get nothing else done. Funny how we take it for granted when life is as Einstein said: "a miracle" and "there are only two ways to live your life. One is as though nothing is a miracle. The other is as though everything is a miracle".

I cannot say that I had been the most grateful person in my entire life. I did not find it easy to be thankful because like most people I didn't see it as a big deal and to be honest I didn't get it. I had assumed it was merely a question of saying thank you when someone brought you something. That may be a coffee, a gift, a card, lunch, dinner, held the elevator door open as I rushed to catch it before it went to the 29th floor and never to be seen again (if that was you, then thank you). Alternatively, let me go before them in the queue because I was in a rush (and if that was you, thank you, I appreciated it). That attitude quickly changed due to some things which I learnt along the way and also as a result of researching what gratitude meant in my own life.

6 UNGRATEFUL

"be grateful for what you have and stop complaining – it bores everyone else, does you no good and doesn't solve any problems".
Zig Ziglar

A funny title you may think for a book about gratitude right?. Well, actually, no. We often focus so much on being grateful, why we should be grateful and what grateful people do and how they behave. The flip side, and perhaps a little neglected side, is that of being ungrateful. It is not something we look at because I guess it doesn't sound attractive or is as beautiful as gratefulness, right?. Even now, something may have stirred up for you. It could be a memory when you were told to be grateful or asked "why aren't you grateful"?, am I right?.

Have you ever asked yourself what the big deal is?, is it a big deal?, should I care? Alternatively, perhaps you pretend to be grateful even though you don't feel it. You pretend to be grateful to avoid people judging you. Maybe you don't 'get' what it is that you are supposed to be thankful for and why. If you have been nodding in agreement to all those questions, I bet my bottom dollar that you would be ticked off if you gave someone a gift, helped them out or lent them something and they did not acknowledge and show their appreciation. Am I right or am I right?. So often that is exactly how we behave. It may be a small gesture of kindness, or it may be an extravagant one. The size is not the point. The point is, are you appreciative of what you already have? Are you even aware of what you have?. So when given more, are you overwhelmed with gratitude knowing full well that what comes quickly to you may not come so easily to others.

Let's be honest often the things we get in life; we don't even necessarily deserve (oooooooooh, I know sounds hardcore and it is). Seriously though, take a moment and think about it. What makes you more worthy of having eyes or legs or parents or the education you have, or a roof over your head, the food you eat or the water you drink, or ....?. You fill in the blank.

I did nothing to deserve the kind parents or siblings that I have, the education, the food, the clean water, the roof over my head. I did nothing to earn or had a right to two legs, two arms, two eyes, two ears. I didn't earn a right to be born. I can tell you though, that I am sure grateful

I was born though. Oprah Winfrey, Tony Robbins, Denzel Washington amongst others talk about grace when they talk about all that they have and the goodness that has and continues to come into their lives. Many successful people understand this at a deeper level, not just at thought level. Many people intellectualise it so much until it doesn't even make sense to themselves. It only becomes some concept even they don't believe or understand. At least it sounds good and makes them seem smart. Do you know what I mean? Is that what you do?

Charles Dickens, Albert Einstein, Fred De Witt Van Amburgh and Jim Rohn amongst many others agree that "true poverty is not being grateful". Sometimes it takes a little bit of time to notice as you reflect on all the little things that you have to be grateful for and never really seen as you rushed through life. Often it is said that it is the little things that bring us joy and that possibly may be true as we look back and see all those little things were pretty big things after all. Again at the time, we didn't notice them as they seemed so insignificant and appeared not to be worthy of praise, appreciation and gratitude. An example of little things is maybe learning first aid, learning to create a fire without matches, learning about all the poisonous plants, memorising your multiple times table at school, having to learn a language at school, learning geometry, learning how to use a compass or read a map, or how to swim.

On a personal note, I confess there were many things I did not understand at the time of why they were needed or why I was required to undertake them. I am grateful though for so many small things because I realise there are no little things. Where I used to work, we had a gardener who naturally was very fond of plants. I occasionally I helped do a bit of gardening which gave me a chance to eat the freshest fruit and veg while soaking up the rays of summer. My job was to root out the weeds amongst the vegetables to give them more space to grow. After a while, Hans Gustav trotted over in his size 14 wellies and saw that I had left the plants with the beautiful black shiny berries growing amongst the vegetables. I thought the berries were edible. They were bright and very delicious looking .after all. They were not edible. Suffice to say a small piece of information possibly saved my life.

Many years later as I saw the same plant and was about to pick the shiny looking berry to eat. I recalled it was the plant that Hans Gustav warned me was not for human consumption. It was belladonna which is often used for medicinal purposes but is poisonous if digested. Who knew, right? The local gardener did thankfully.

Have you ever sat with someone or heard someone complain about how awful their life is?. Don't tell me you haven't because I am going to call you a big fat liar. I know you have. So admit it. Maybe your not accepting it because it's you who does all the complaining. Am I right or am I right?. When we are consistently doing that, it is unbecoming. Secondly, it puts people off. I mean who wants to be around someone who is utterly blind to what they do have and can only see the faults in others day in day out. Earlier on we discussed the example of the woman who had everything but, was still complaining. Those who saw her could not understand why she was not happy and could not be at least be grateful for all that she had. Compared to an average person because she had a heck of a lot. You may be able to listen to someone complain about a daily basis, but most people cannot and don't want to.

As a result of having met a few similar people in different circles, it struck me that these people indeed were unaware of all the good in their lives. It wasn't necessarily clear at first whether they cared or not; however, it did become apparent shortly after that. Their lack of gratitude showed up in their friendships, in their relationships, in their families, in the neighbourhood and their jobs. Perhaps the Roman Lucius Annaeus Seneca said it best when he said: "nothing is more honourable than a grateful heart."

Grateful people share and don't fear lack because they know there is plenty for everyone so aren't stingy or miserly or greedy. Instead, they are giving of themselves and their resources, and do so happily and freely. Author Jack Canfield who speaks and writes extensively has shared what his mentor W. Clement Stone taught him., Clement stated that "if you are thankful, what do you do? You share". W. Clement Stone doesn't mention the particular kinds of sharing. The sharing could be your time, your money, your resources, your knowledge, your expertise, your name or brand amongst so many other things that you may wish to donate. Some forms of sharing may be more natural than others. Do you know which areas you find easy to give from and which areas you struggle? Write them down below.

....

....

....

....

....

....

Some of us find sharing certain things more comfortable than others. You may find it easier to give away your time rather than donate money. It may be easier for you to donate your old unwanted goods rather than volunteer your time to a charity or raise money for a particular cause.

The following story is an example of giving to look good. It is an example whereby the giving is not from gratitude and the awareness of all that the individual already has.

Christmas often viewed as a time of generosity and giving. It is not necessarily a time of giving the same gifts to many people in the neighbourhood: the gift, a simple box of chocolates from the high street — the same chocolates sent to 20 of the local neighbours. The intention was not giving out of gratitude, appreciation or possibly even kindness. As a result, these 20 boxes of chocolates were not authentic gifts. Instead, they were boxes of chocolates given to 20 people to make the giver look good, giving, kind and charitable. The focus was on looking good. The expectation was on reciprocation, i.e. to receive 20 gifts back. So the moral of the story, yes, you guessed it, and I am sure your parents told you too, and that is don't give to receive. The funny thing about gratitude is that it cannot be anything but authentic.

Giving gifts out to others to receive back is not true giving. It is better not to give than give and expect a gift of similar or higher value in return. It is instead giving from the overflow and abundance that you have that W. Clement Stone refers. It may not necessarily be as easy as we think to genuinely provide or share, mainly if the motive is to get something back in return. Unfortunately not receiving like for like, or more than what you gave combined with the need to look good results in a game of self-justification, resentment, blaming others and making them wrong for not reciprocating. The American Jewish writer, professor, political activist, Nobel Laureate, and Holocaust survivor, Elie Wiesel said: "when someone doesn't have gratitude, something is missing in his or her humanity".

German psychoanalyst, Karen Horney highlighted many of us have a "tyranny of should" and how rigid and inflexible the inner dialogue can be (don't start thinking you haven't got one. It is that voice in your head that you cannot turn off. The one that is probably telling you now there is no such thing as the voice in your head. Yes, everyone has it and so do you). It is the mountain of shoulds that create the stress and guilt; for example, "I should be perfect", "I should be thin", "I should be successful". Horney encouraged her patients to develop a subtle change in the words and language used to express themselves. She highlighted that the subtle change "nuances in their vocabulary" would assist them in creating a better fit between the inner words they use to tell themselves how it should be and reality. Horney found that this simple measure used frequently improved patients moods.

Gratefulness is not saying thank you and rushing out to buy like for like or outdoing people with their gifts. Keeping up with the Joneses would not exist if we were grateful because we would appreciate what we have rather than focus on what we don't have. The grass would appear just as green in our back yard.

The funny thing is we all know what Charles Schwab (the man who worked for steel magnate Andrew Carnegie), the Dalai Lama, philosopher and psychologist William James said to ring true, i.e. "the deepest craving of human nature is the need to be appreciated". We all struggle, you may be struggling right now to see, what you have that you can appreciate, right now. Moreover, therein lies the issue. You are looking for things to give you gratitude. Your waiting for someone to give you something, do something for you so you feel loved and appreciated and then you can smile and say "thanks". Well, that is not gratitude. That's just you wanting stuff, or wanting someone to do something for you and then getting it, then saying "thanks". Rather like ungratefulness is a way of being, gratefulness is a way of being. You may be thinking that you are owed, or earned and have every given right to have the things you have.

I am sure you do, however, imagine everything taken from you, or burnt down, or flooded. What would you say to yourself and others?. How would you speak about what happened?. Brene Brown, a research professor at The Graduate College of Social Work at the University of Houston on talking about gratitude says "what separates privilege from entitlement is gratitude. While Robbs, yes Tony Robbins highlights that "when you are grateful, fear disappears and abundance appears".

Often it is said and has been told throughout the ages by many, including the Greek philosophers that our deepest fears all relate to the fear of death. The two existential fears are aloneness and death, and it is to these that all our fears and anxieties link.

German psychoanalyst, Karen Horney and American social researcher Brene Brown both talk about vulnerability and examine the lives of those who have gone through tremendous amounts of stress and trauma. Horney found that often people had breakdowns because of events that were stressful and these events collided with and didn't bode well with their vulnerabilities. While Brown discovered in her research the surprising fact that many of those very people who had gone through great difficulties such as genocide and were trauma survivors, experienced the death of someone close, parents whose child died, were filled with gratitude. Those who shared their stories recommended that which has discussed throughout this book, which is don't take things for granted. Furthermore, the research participants recommended not only not to take it for granted but share your gratitude and also celebrate it. These same participants like many advocates of gratitude practised gratitude rather than merely feel the feelings of gratefulness or have an attitude of gratitude as some call it.

Frank Tallis, a clinical psychologist and author discusses in his work what he has discovered amongst his patients over and over again, that is that crises are catalysts; "they move us on, break us up, so we can meet in new forms". As a result of undergoing extreme pain or difficulty, people have become more grateful rather than ungrateful. They reminded themselves of what they had and created possibilities for themselves and their lives. It takes work and is not necessarily an overnight process. It started with an intention, backed up by continuous action and picking themselves up each time they fell. They focused on the road ahead rather than on the past in the rear-view mirror.

Sometimes even grateful people need to be reminded to stop being ungrateful as they forget to recognise and express their gratitude for the things they have. Since we started with a straight from the hip shooting quote from motivational speaker and author, Zig Ziglar, let's end with another one of his straight from the hip shooting quotes. The left hip this time.

"The more you recognise and express gratitude for the things you have, the more things you will have to express gratitude for"

7 WHAT GRATITUDE LOOKS LIKE

"Thankfulness is the beginning of gratitude . Gratitude is the completion of thankfulness. Thankfulness may consist merely of words. Gratitude is shown in acts"
Henri Fredric Amiel

Gratitude is not just about saying thank you as a routine but feeling the feelings of it. It is deeper, more profound. It's a genuine feeling of knowing you have not done anything to deserve or have earned the gift and yet you were given it out of grace, out of love by the other and it's the sheer overwhelming feeling of appreciation. If it was indeed about how great people or how worthy they were, none of us would deserve anything. A neighbour of mine from Zimbabwe, a lawyer, ended up coming to the UK in the hope of improving his life and after many jobs, most people would consider lowly he ended up working as a dustbin man for the local authority. I have never seen someone more appreciative for what he had had in Zimbabwe (a lot) and what he had in the UK (a little). Unless you knew him, you would have never guessed how much he had given up. He did count his blessings. He was genuinely grateful not only for what he had in terms of stuff but on a deeper level. Many would have felt anger, resentment, resignation at having to do so many menial jobs as a qualified lawyer. He was forced to leave his home country and start all over again as a dustbin man. Back home he was never seen without wearing one of his expensive suits. He lived in a large house with his family surrounded by a tight-knit community of friends and relatives.

It was my neighbour's whole way of being and his grateful attitude to life. It was truly humbling and yet at the same time remarkably inspiring to watch. It was even more impacting when I heard the full extent his life back home. It sounded idyllic, and the exact opposite of everything he now had.

Scholar, Ibn Qayyim Al – Jawziyyah wrote that "if gratitude was merely lip service and not expressed by the rest of the body it was similar to a man who touched a piece of clothing but did not wear it. So it did not protect him from the different elements".

Jawziyyah highlights how one can show the gratitude of the eyes, the gratitude of the ears, gratitude of the hands, gratitude of the head, gratitude of the sexual organs. In essence, he discusses how praising that which is good and leaving alone that which is not beneficial. The gratitude of the hands, for example, is not taking that which is not yours and helping others who have less than you, or need help but may not necessarily ask for it. The gratitude of the head is maybe having knowledge, wisdom or understanding and sharing it. The gratitude of the sexual organs is perhaps refraining when and where necessary although you may desire to or wish to have it. Will Smith (Actor, father, musician-producer, songwriter and comedian) says it how it is, i.e. refraining from going out with your cousin's girl, although you may want to.

There is an old story of two men, both of whom had been given much and had accumulated considerable wealth. One of the men had ended up losing everything, and yet he still kept thanking his lord, still kept being grateful, even when they took his bed. Meanwhile, the other man was taken aback by this man who had lost everything and yet was still appreciative. It did not make sense. Why would someone be praising his lord when he had lost everything?. He couldn't see anything to be thankful or appreciative for as he imagined himself in the other man's shoes. So sounding perplexed, he asked the man why he was grateful and still praising his lord? The one who had lost everything told him that he was thankful for all that he had. It was worth more than anything anyone could offer him. He added that no matter how much someone tried to give him for what he still had he would never give them all his blessings. Now the other man was curious. What could they be he wondered and thought if he too could get them. So the first man told him, feeling astonished that it was not already abundantly clear. He was thanking and praising his lord for the blessings of eyesight, his hearing, his hands, his ability to walk, his ability to think, and so on.............

Sometimes we get so wrapped up in words. We often focus, and it all just becomes a nice theory as we shout "Next" for another approach to occupying us. We become entangled in the giving and taking or just the taking or just the giving so much that we forget what we already have. It quickly becomes just another thing we quote to others, tell others to do and talk about at events and gatherings we attend. We suddenly re-remember when we read the next book, go to the next do, seminar or course, or lecture. No one wants to admit that they don't want to have to do the work. It is even more so at present in an era of high tech where demands are constant and its full speed ahead. Everyone would rather have the benefits of gratitude instantaneously without the work. It doesn't work like that. Deep down, you know that though. First, you do the work, i.e. first you become aware, become grateful. Then put that gratitude into practice to gain the full benefits of gratitude that the science highlights.

Often you will find that people don't voice their gratitude for their blessings. However, the very same people are quick to complain about what they don't have and "look at Deborah and Ross. They have so much. Of course, they are grateful, I mean look at them, look how much they have. If I had so much, I would be grateful, every day". Sound familiar?. Of course, it sounds familiar. If you are honest, you will find you do that yourself (I saw you nodding your head, saying yes. Yes you agree you do that). We all do when we don't get what we want, or feel we deserve it, and someone else has it and why don't we. It makes sense then, if you cannot be grateful for the little things, you most definitely won't be thankful for the big stuff when they come along. Sometimes the most beautiful things are the things created from a struggle, like a pearl, inside the oyster shell. It is not a single pearl a necklace makes rather a collection of many pearls, put together on a string. See each pearl as a blessing which one day became a bigger blessing and turned into a beautiful necklace.

Are you someone who doesn't say thank you to people when they do something or give something to you?. Alternatively, do you mumble "thank you" half-heartedly as if it is a chore?.

Someone compliments you on the cufflinks, the dress, the shoes or how dapper you look. You can see they genuinely mean it but you brush it off quickly and start saying "oh this dress it is old, had it for years, it doesn't really suit me anymore, I should really give it to the charity shop" or regarding looking smart you say "what are you saying I don't always look smart"?. Whereas a simple "thank you" would have sufficed the other person is left wondering why they complimented you. They are unlikely to do so in the future.

Now imagine it is not enough that you do that with friends, colleagues and socially but you also do that day in and day out at home. Imagine the impact you are having on your family, your partner, your children. Seriously think about that for a moment. At work or socially when someone buys you a drink, or your invited to dinner and they make you dinner, you say "thank you". They bring you dessert, you say "thank you", they make you a coffee, you say "thank you". If they pour you a glass of water, you say "thank you". Someone passes you the bread basket; you say "thank you". Someone passes you the Salad dish you say "thank you". Someone serves you a spoonful of rice or meat from the main dish you say "thank you". Someone passes you the mayonnaise or ketchup you say "thank you". All the time the thank you is accompanied by a smile. Meanwhile at home, if your partner, child, sibling or any other family member brings you a cup of tea, you take it for granted and sound more like a grizzly bear. It could be that you do say thank you to the larger family, just not to your partner and kids. Sounding familiar?

We become blind to our actions and are quick to complain about what others don't do, and yet others are continually doing for us, but we don't see it. Sometimes we don't want to. We measure and reserve our thanks for the big things that we feel deserve our thanks. We don't want to be throwing around our gratitude, in case people think we are incapable and weak right? Often those who do thank people will not thank God.

"You will be enriched in every way so that you can be generous on every occasion and through us your generosity will result in thanksgiving to God"
(Corinthians 9:11)

"If you are grateful I will add more favours upon you"
(Ibrahim 14:7)

"...all this is for your benefit, so that the grace that is reaching more and more people may cause thanksgiving to overflow to the glory of God" (Corinthians 4:15-16)
""Enter his gates with thanksgiving and his courts with praise; give thanks to him and praise his name (God)"
(Psalm 100:4)

".....And swiftly we shall reward those that serve us with gratitude" (Al Imran 3:145) .....and be grateful to God if it is him you worship" (Al Baqarah 2:172)

Mother Theresa upon discussing gratitude said, "the best way to show my gratitude to God is to accept everything, even my problems with joy". In essence, Mother Theresa echoed the words from the Bible in Philippians 4: 6-8 and in Thessalonians 5:18, "in everything give thanks". German writer and philosopher, Gotthold Ephraim Lessing and 13th-century Persian poet Rumi said the same thing, in different words. Lessing said, "a single grateful thought toward heaven is the most complete prayer". In comparison, Rumi highlighted "if you only say one prayer in a day, make it thank you". There are many versions of these sayings throughout the ages. Socrates, Victor Hugo, Epictetus, Abu Bakr, William Shakespeare, Charles Dickens and Ralph Waldo Emerson amongst many, many others all reinforce the importance of and power of gratitude in our daily lives.

You may be someone who does not believe in a creator, a higher power, greater than yourself. You may feel that these quotes apply to you, or that these men and women of history and even today are related to religion. Perhaps they are and perhaps they are not. Ask yourself though if you are not happy where you are right now, is it not worth at least trying this practice out?. It doesn't cost you anything. It may take up a little bit of your time which you may have spent watching a rerun of a show you didn't want to watch. So what's the harm in trying?. As Thomas A. Edison said, "discontent is the first necessity of progress". Furthermore, Eleanor Roosevelt stated that "you should do one thing every day that scares you". If you really cannot wait, jump to chapter 11 to learn about the gratitude journal so you can jump into action today and start practising.

8 GRATITUDE AND WORK

"Gratitude also opens your eyes to the limitless potential of the universe, while dissatisfaction closes your eyes to it"
Stephen Richards

If you use any form of social media be that Twitter, Facebook, Instagram, LinkedIn or any other you will notice the number of comments or articles on a weekly or monthly basis regarding work. The comments are not necessarily positive. Often it is the very people who are working at the organisation criticising the organisation and their colleagues. The lack of gratitude between and by staff is one of the primary drivers in people taking time off, being absent, long term sickness, job dissatisfaction, staff turnover, stress and overwhelm resulting in early retirement or long term health issues and possible burnout.

If your an employee when was the last time you thanked your colleagues?. A genuine heartfelt thank you. Not one of those when someone passed you a pen, and you mumbled "hmm thanks" while on the phone to a customer. As an employee when did you last thank your manager or anyone in the managerial team?. (many of you I am sure made that comment mean something more than it is. It may have caused you to react, and thereby the internal chatter has gone off about why should you?. Why have you got to thank them?.You are after all doing the work for them. Am I right or am I right?).

If you are a manager when was the last time you genuinely showed your appreciation and expressed your gratitude to your colleagues and staff?. When did you thank other managers in your team and those in the organisation? You may be thinking that is what the senior management team should be doing. Do you think that?. The more time you spend time considering what others should be doing, the more time, in essence, you are staying stuck in being ungrateful. Unconsciously and maybe consciously you are unwilling or feel incapable of being grateful. As a result to continue to play small and complain about others who are down in the arena getting messy but also gaining. All the while you sit in the stands as a spectator wondering when someone will lift you?. When someone will notice you?. When will someone pick you to join the winning dream team?. When will someone make you feel great and say thank you?. It's the difference of being a gladiator, tennis player, football player, basketball player on the court and a spectator dressed in the team's t-shirt criticising his team who are giving their all on the court. The stands are safe because you avoid getting involved. You also avoid the reaping the rewards of a heart that is genuinely grateful because you wish not to give.

You want others to give first, and then you will start thanking and giving to others. You argue with anyone who dares to tell you otherwise as you dazzle them with your brilliant analytical mind. You are determined to prove them all wrong rather than try to be grateful. Does that sound like you?. It may be that you are not like that at all deep down. Is it possible that you have given a lot and you got burnt?. Did you give people your time, money, loyalty, years of your life only to find they never appreciated it and left you utterly bewildered as to what went wrong?. You now feel you cannot trust anyone. You are determined to make everyone pay for the mistake your ex-wife, your ex-husband, your business partner, your children, or your neighbour made. They were not grateful, and you gave them everything. You are now giving no one anything anymore. Sound more like your situation?

Adam Grant, Author of 'Give and Take' and Harvard researcher Francesca Gino undertook research that highlighted that for people to continue supporting you they needed to help to be recognised. Furthermore when an individual wasn't shown gratitude their desire to help you again decreased instantly to less than 50%.

A manager of mine once told me when I newly joined his team; "remember if one finger is pointing at you, four are pointing back at the person. In all honesty, I found it amusing and thought it as just another one his anecdotes. He would often be making jokes and telling us funny stories. He was renowned for his northern accent and sense of humour in the office. I did learn as I progressed throughout my career what he meant with that simple but profound statement. I often found myself quoting him. I will and am forever grateful for his stories and reminding me there is enough to talk about rather than talk about other people by finding faults in them regularly. He was an avid reader and always had a highlighter in his rucksack or in his hand ready to highlight one of the many books he read.

It's funny how easy we find it to complain about people and yet so often we struggle to show our appreciation and gratitude towards the very people we are in contact with daily.

Gratitude has many benefits including strengthening relationships. Recent research shows that when you express your appreciation to another person, it helps to strengthen and create a closer and longer lasting relationship in comparison to relationships with someone who is ungrateful. People want to make time and put in the effort for those who are grateful and express it.

We all know someone, or maybe we are that someone who is ungrateful. That lack of gratitude quickly discolours an otherwise good relationship. Often the constant complaining and gossiping is merely a guise for our lack of appreciation for all that we do have. A tactic we use to avoid having to look in the mirror because if we do, we may have to transform those habits and do some work on ourselves to change. That would mean having to confront our behaviour. I am sure I have triggered something within you. If I have and you feel angry, annoyed, or judged, good. Yes, good. As long as you recognised and acknowledged your feeling that right now, it is good. Be honest, be honest; that is how you are feeling. Be honest that you do get involved in gossip and complaining and how it makes you feel. It does make you feel good. It may give you a buzz, a high, that you know something from the grapevine before others do, or how people trust you, so they tell you things. It is not about shaming you or making you feel guilty, instead, this is about recognising and being honest with yourself that you do gossip and that there is a 'payoff' like a junkie who gets a kick from the drug as it enters his system. If you didn't get some pleasure you would not do it or get involved in it, would you?. You need to see the pattern you are living in and be aware of what you are doing and be honest with yourself why you do it.

You may be sitting there thinking everyone gossips, and everyone complains. Why does it matter?. It shouldn't matter. It doesn't matter. Why doesn't she change?. why doesn't he change?. You don't know my workplace. You don't understand what kind of people I work. You don't see the boss I have to put up with or any other reason you are thinking of right now. Those things may all be correct; however, is there a level of resentment and resignation for it all?. Do you point and blame others for how you are and where you are in your job, your life?. Do you take responsibility for your role of where you are?. Alternatively, is it all everyone else's fault that you are not happy?. Is that why you don't want to practice gratitude?. Is that why you don't feel you cannot be grateful for anything? Is that why you gossip, out of boredom, to distract yourself?.

Have you ever thought that the people your gossiping about and what they did, with who, what, how and where, they will, very likely and eventually gossip about you?.

Ok, so you may be wondering how to convert a negative quality into a positive one. Great question if you are. Often there is a lack of gratitude at work, so you will find yourself involved in gossiping and complaining while also wanting what others have. As a result, we steal peoples respect, their time, their energy, while wanting their job or their salary.

You need to be more than just aware by being honest with yourself that you have this pattern of behaviour, and see the way it pans out in your life before you can transform it. Don't worry about others being ungrateful. As Gandhi said to his followers "be the change you want to see". It's not about beating yourself up. Now that you see your habit, it is an opportunity to create a new possibility. You can use the problem to your advantage, to create something better. I know, it suddenly got exciting. Right? (nod your head, so I feel better, knowing you are still with me, nod it a bit more. Great, that's better).

So now that I have your curiosity let's answer it. You can turn your tendency for complaining and gossiping into a new possibility by assisting the very people you are gossiping about (I know for many of you those very words have stirred up some feelings and now the choir inside you is going at full volume. That is ok too). The same energy you are using to complain and gossip could be used to build others up. You could find a way to use all the disadvantages that you feel that keep showing up, and make yourself stronger and more potent by channelling all your negative energy and pain and time into being more creative and focusing on giving to others. As you help others and volunteer your time to projects, teams and those junior to you, you will notice you become more interested in others. As you become more interested in others, you will see that the very person you gossiped about, thought you were superior to, whom you thought didn't like you, whom you didn't like, thought was weak, angry, uneducated, too educated, a smart Alec, unkind, a narcissist, obnoxious, rude, out of touch with reality and so son. You will find they are, in fact, none of those things. You may well discover that the reel you had running in your head about them, really was just that, i.e. a reel within your movie, where you were the director, executioner and judge and there was only one way, one view, i.e. yours. When we go to the cinema, we are so interested and want to get to know the main character, get inside their head to understand them, we read them and want to know more. Your very weaknesses can become your strengths.

Ok, lets come back to gratitude at work and discuss gossip and complaining further in the next chapter. Let's do an exercise to take a look at what's going on. In the table below write down what it is that you want and if possible why. It may be that you wish to have your colleague's job because you feel they get paid more. They get more perks in their role than you do. Alternatively, it may be that they get a business car and you don't. They get to go on business trips, to conferences, shows and get a chance to network. They have more responsibility and more power than you do or any other number of things that come to mind.

Now write down all the things that you have and experience currently in your job that invokes gratitude. If you find yourself thinking nothing, try thinking of the benefits. You may want to start with the simple fact that you get paid each month to do your job. Start with something you probably take for granted such as, water to make a tea/coffee, maybe you get free milk, sugar and tea/coffee.   Is it the generous pension plan, with company contributions?. It may be all the free training, information and expertise you have onsite. The learning may not be in the form of external courses; however, many people within the organisation have a great deal of knowledge. They are experts in their field from whom you could learn from if you wanted to. What qualities do you see in the person who does the job you want to do?.

Next, write down how you aim to acquire more or similar skills. You notice that the job that you want to do requires particular expertise. The awareness of and the ability to use specific software, which you currently don't have. How will you go about learning it?. Have you asked the person who is presently doing the job for help?. Have you asked advice from family, friends, colleagues or people in your network for help?. Many people are happy to help and share their knowledge and expertise. You may be pleasantly surprised by asking. The person you are requesting to teach you the new skill will be grateful you have asked and be more than happy you asked as highlighted by Kenneth Blanchard in the 'One Minute Manager' and the hilarious 'Year of Yes' by Shonda Rhimes.

Shonda allowed herself to open up following a chat with her sister who had told her she always said "no" to pretty much everything. As a result of that conversation and determination to keep her word Shonda discovered a whole new world of possibilities as she started to say yes to life. If you want further proof, read Katie Byron's 'Loving What is' and 'Who Would You Be Without Your Story'. Katie's works will help you discover it is you who is stopping you and the stories you tell yourself. Katei echoes the words of Tony Robbin's mentor Jim Rohn who highlighted the importance of being grateful and seeing the good in where you are to move to where you want to.

what you want?	Why you want it?	Grateful I for in the current role	Action to acquire skills

9 GOSSIP AND COMPLAINING

"you cannot give what you do not have."
Thomas Troward

The two words somehow don't seem to sit well together, do they?. That is because they don't. Another word to put in place of gossip would be ungrateful or ingratitude.

Peter Bregman, the author of "18 Minutes" and "Four Seconds," talks about many things that he has encountered in business, socially and within family life. Peter discusses how counteracting someone who is complaining and gossiping with your positivity; in essence, their negativity "doesn't work because it is argumentative. Peter adds that "people don't like to be emotionally contradicted, and if you try to convince them that they shouldn't feel something, they'll only feel it more stubbornly."

He goes on to say that the alternative doesn't work either. Another, more natural option would be to join in with the complaining and gossiping, i.e. their negativity. It doesn't work and only makes it worse.

Beneath all of the gossip, complaining and negativity is a deep need to be understood. Often the same people want to be heard are struggling with a lack of gratitude. You may do this yourself or find this at work or in your social groups. I may include housemates, friends, families, groups you work with or volunteer. People will complain about others who are different, who don't share their views or values, interests, ambitions or goals. Instead of being grateful for the differences and acknowledge our feelings we tend to point out what is wrong in the other person quickly. We stand around in the kitchen, go to a quiet meeting room, go outside for a smoke with others, sit in the canteen, anywhere away from the people we are discussing. Some of us are brave enough to sit in an open plan office and complain about others. We do this as leaders and managers.

Instead of listening to our staff we complain about others, by showing them, we are not interested in hearing to others. We only value them until they do something for us to gossip or become a cause for complaint. Then we won't appreciate them either. In essence, we express our lack of gratitude, by constantly complaining, and not recognising peoples other qualities apart from the one that frustrates us.

It is the regular expression of gratitude by senior management to their staff that has a positive effect on productivity by increasing it, generating creativity and stimulating cooperation amongst people and teams.

As we all know emotions both positive and negative can affect the whole team, other teams, the entire organisation, families and communities. Feelings can have a contagious effect. Emmons and McCullough's book "The Psychology of Gratitude" talks about how positive emotions such as gratitude, joy, inspiration and love amongst others seem to have the ability to transform people, communities and companies. These positive feelings grow as a result of people connecting, creating meaningful relationships, communities and companies that work at higher levels.

So what has this all got to do with gossip and complaining, you may think. In essence, it is all linked. If you tend to start or get involved in rumours, whereby you are merely complaining and creating negative space, you are acting ungrateful. It may sound hard. You may not even realise that you are gossiping or how much of your time is spent doing it. It may be second nature to you, and you may not even recognise the impact it has on you.

It can be draining and who genuinely finds it an attractive trait in people or wants to spend time with people who waste so much time doing so?. As someone who works in the private and the public sector, I get the chance to meet people from many different backgrounds. I will find myself drawn to those who are grateful. Grateful people tend to know they are enough and have enough. They have no qualms in sharing their time, helping you connect, being vulnerable, making friends, sharing what they know. They want you to succeed rather than hold you back or be envious. They are relaxed, resilient friendly and interested in hearing about the good rather than getting involved in gossiping and playing being small. Author, Joyce Meyers highlighted how when you complain, you remain in the same situation. You continually focus on the same things and go round and round.

Why gratitude and gossiping don't go hand in hand is because when you are genuinely grateful and practising gratitude, you are saying I am enough. You can forgive. You see people where they are and realise that you cannot give something away that you do not possess. You can only love others to the extent that you love yourself. You cannot be grateful, understanding, compassionate, forgiving towards others because you do not possess those attributes yourself and are not practising them for yourself. You are saying that you are not enough and neither are other people. As a result, you gossip, fall into the blame game, make others wrong and end up never talking to the other person. Alternatively, you do speak to the other person, but from a judgmental standpoint which the other person senses.

Instead of creating connection and relating to others you do anything to avoid confrontation. You skirt around the issue and resort to talking to your close colleagues at work, to your friends and family. You avoid bringing up the real problem with the person you are gossiping about to others. As a result, you create stories that almost turn into a never seen before drama that any film director in any industry would be amazed. Any movie industry such as the likes of Hollywood, Bollywood, Tollywood (Telugu film industry), Kollywood (Tamil film industry), Pollywood (Pakistan and India Punjabi language only), Lollywood or Kariwood (Pakistan film industry), Chollywod or Dhollywood (Indian film industry), Mollywood, Sandalwood, Jollywood, Ollywood, Sollywood, Dhaliwood (Bangladesh film industry), Ghollywood (Ghana's film industry), Nollywood (Nigeran movie industry). Riverwood (Kenya's film industry), Swahiliwood (Tanzania's film industry), Ugawood (Uganda's film industry), Zollywood (Zimbabwe's film industry), Mollywood (Mormon film industry in America) or perhaps into Hallyuwood (South Korean film industry).

Is it possible that your industry did not get mentioned ?. Is your story is soooooo unique that you think there should be a new genre?. Alternatively, is your self composed script a mixture of all of the world's movies and dramas that would give the Greek tragedies a run for their money?.

The more you complain and gossip about people and things the more you will have to complain. In essence, what you resist persists. You will find yourself drawn to people who gossip and complain, and it may not be possible to avoid them. Peter Bregman suggests that instead of getting involved with the gossip to acknowledge and validate people where they are. As a result, you don't avoid the situation neither get heavily involved.

It is hard to see the positive in people who constantly gossip, which may be nasty. Now I am not saying the next bit is going to be easy. No. What I am saying though, is that it is possible.

I am perhaps more aware of gossiping and complaining that I should be. It is because I do many projects for many different companies and travel a lot. As a result, I get to work with every kind of people and company which I enjoy. The downside is that of trying not to get pulled into the office gossip, who doesn't like who, who has done what with whom and when who doesn't do what and the list goes on and on. I listened and listened and listened and listened and listened and then listened some more. It did beg the question of how one person could talk so much or have so much to say. It soon became clear why they spoke about the issue and why they did not go and speak to the person they were complaining about directly. Their gossip was an accumulation of stories they had made up in their heads about the other person. Each time the other person said or did something the individual took that to mean something. They were thereby adding another layer to the story in their head about the person. As a result, all that the individual could see was someone who didn't care, or listen to them. In turn, it caused unnecessary conflict internally and externally for both individuals.

Instead of going back and talking to the person from a different viewpoint, the individual will avoid doing anything that causes pain, fearing conflict. As human beings, we try our best to avoid pain wherever possible and would much rather seek pleasure. As a result, we enjoy telling stories to friends, other co-workers and family. It helps to avoid conflict and creates joy from creating sympathy from others who rally around taking sides against the other person. It then becomes them versus us: queue the Montagues and Capulets in Romeo and Juliet.

You may laugh and think who would do that?. Rather like an addict, the gossiper will keep going back to the story and keep adding to it, making it more tender and juicer, hooking others into their drama. It may start as something small; for example, your colleague did not greet you at work in the morning. It may be that your colleague didn't listen to you and added the wrong pictures into the final print and it went out in the company name to a perspective and well-known client that you have wanted to do business with for many years. Instead of resolving the situation first, by talking to the client and working with your colleague to amend the error, you speak to the client and ignore your colleague. You cannot believe how this happened or why they would do this to you?

You feel like something is wrong, your being punished and quickly become the victim in the story. You complain to others how incompetent your colleague is. You cannot believe how you are going to tell the client whilst also try and fix the problem. You forget the colleague who is more than likely devastated and will also now create a story of what it all means and tell colleagues, friends and family. As a result, both people are gossiping about each other. As a result of the total breakdown in communication, there is tension instead of a possibility. By remaining in that state, creativity remains stifled, and nothing new can appear. It will take something from you to transform the situation.

So what can be done instead of gossiping and complaining about others? The next chapter talks about some practical things you can put into practice to help. In situations like these apart from forgiving, overlooking peoples mistakes and being in communication, is to practice gratitude. Be grateful for the negative, the things that go wrong, the people you can't stand or wind you up when you say "yes" when you want to say "no" or something much stronger. Be grateful that these people who came into your life even though you may feel they had or are having an adverse effect.

There is always the flip side which funnily enough is the title of the book by Author, Adam Jackson. It looks at the situation from a different perspective. The flip side may be that the very people you are complaining and gossiping about are holding up a mirror to you. They are showing you that the very areas you don't like in others and are quick to complain about, are the areas or things you don't like about yourself. They are showing you a mirror and showing you that you have a choice. You can look back at yourself in the mirror. See yourself, and the areas that have been made apparent to you that you don't like in others. Those very things you don't want in others, also exist in you, and you don't like them in yourself. So focus on them. Work on them. (I am sure the whole choir in your head is singing and not necessarily in harmony right now. Right? Are you trying to ignore or bypass what we are talking about because you feel it doesn't apply to you? Did you mumble "no"?. You big fat liar. If your human it applies to you. Remember we are friends so we can talk straight, right? Do you want a friend who lies to you?. No, right?. You can do this, and once you do, I want to hear about it so write to me and tell me how it has changed your life. Ok. (nod your head, so I know your still there, not singing with the choir. Ok. Good. You did nod right?. I am trusting you. Ok, nod a bit stronger this time, so I see it. That's better. Thanks).

Ok, come back to the mirror. It is a chance for you to see the qualities that exist in you, but you don't necessarily see in yourself. Maybe I am wrong and you do see but thus far you have chosen to ignore what you see because it hurts, you don't like to, or it is out right easier not to dig in case you hit the pipe and find an unstoppable geyser. Yes like the ones in the movies when they hit oil and bingo a never ending geyser supply of crude oil in the desert. Instead, you see the parts of you that you don't like, reflected in others to you, and it irritates you, you try to change the other person, but cannot change them. You never look at yourself and see you are a reflection of what you see in the other person and keep complaining about day in day out, or whenever you get a chance to blow steam about her or him. Incredible isn't it just. However, the great thing is that it does give you a chance to learn and grow.

The other option is you look in the mirror and see those aspects and ways of being in others you don't like within yourself, and choose to remain the same. You may view all that has been highlighted to you by the people you encounter and struggle as a challenge and do take action to transform the area. You may, on the other hand, choose to do nothing and continue to lead the life you are leading where you remain a spectator, judging others and making them small and making yourself right. As a spectator as Brene Brown says, you have no right to criticise those who are getting hurt because they are living their lives and giving their all in the arena. That takes courage and vulnerability as she points out in her book "Daring Greatly."

You may not find this particularly easy but I can assure you it is beneficial. Take a separate piece of paper or write it in the space below. Try to sit somewhere quiet and write down all the good qualities of the people or person that you make wrong by judging and criticising. If you have found yourself gossiping about a friend or colleague write their name down on the piece of paper, or don't if you instantly start having an adverse reaction. You can add the name later, at the end. Look back at the times when the person your gossiping and complaining about has done something for you. It may be something simple as a smile, a "good morning", "how are you"?, maybe they were making a tea and asked if you wanted one, perhaps they shared a packet of biscuits, donated towards your birthday present, wrote something sweet in your birthday card, asked you if you were ok when you were tired or didn't look well. Write all these things down. Our brains are wired to focus on the negative, almost as if they wouldn't survive without being so. It is, therefore, necessary to practice and not just think about gratitude and being grateful. Instead like when you received a compliment that is quickly forgotten or overridden in seconds when something rude or unkind is said. We remember the negative and promptly forget the positive comment or compliment.

....

....

....

....

....

....

....

....

....

....

....

....

....

....

....

....

....

....

....

....

....

....

....

....

....

....

....

....

Like gratitude has a positive effect on our minds and bodies so too does forgiveness. Therefore learn to let go and forgive so that in turn your misgivings and mistakes may be overlooked. Even more importantly learn to forgive yourself and be grateful for what you have so that out of that what you have you can give to others, be that gratefulness or forgiveness. Learn to appreciate and acknowledge the good in others rather than focus on their shortcomings. Learn to talk about yourself more because truly grateful people are exciting and far too busy to get sucked in with gossiping about others. The reason being they are doing things to help and improve the lives of others. They are too busy working on goals and projects more significant than themselves, more prominent than their workplace or group they hang out with at school, college, university, work, neighbourhood or local community.

Constant complaining, gossiping and being negative blocks gratitude. Like oil and water, the two do not mix regardless of how hard you may try. You cannot complain and be grateful. Both affect every area of your life. One affects you positively and acknowledges the good while the other effects you negatively and accepts all that is wrong. There is always a cause and effect. We all know this intuitively. You choose.

Often you will find that how people behave at home is how they act in their communities, at schools, colleges, universities and work. You may argue that most people gossip, complain and are negative. You may add that they have managed to survive, get on well with people and may even be wealthy. Moreover, those are all good points. However, there is the outward appearance of happiness and the authentic happiness that comes from within when you live with appreciation rather than take everything and everyone for granted.

Many people are stuck and complain about their partner, their wife, their husband, their employees, their colleagues, their managers, their companies, their schools, their colleges, their universities, their friends, their marriage, their mortgage, their business, their neighbours, their ex, their current partner, their children, their income, the excess of hair, the lack of hair, and the never-ending list goes on. You get to choose if you want to focus on the problems or see the opportunities and the goodness within the issues.

Author Don Miguel Ruiz sums all this by stating "when you look in the mirror and hate what you see, you need addictions to survive. If you don't like the main character in your story, then everything and everyone in it becomes a nightmare. However, if you accept 100% then trust yourself. So whatever you manifest in the world will happen.". Ruiz also adds that "nothing people do is because of you. It is because of themselves".

Now that you have written a list highlighting what you appreciate in others that you had previously been complaining about writing one about yourself. Better still write those things that you are appreciative and grateful about in and of yourself, in the space below. If you naturally struggle with seeing your qualities, this is a great exercise. In the first part write the things about yourself that you do every day that you don't appreciate. An example of this may be that you don't listen when people are talking and often interrupt the other person. Perhaps you notice that you tend to be grumpy and short tempered. Maybe your more subtle and tend not to say anything and hold it all in. You get the gist. Keep it simple and don't make a whole story out of it. Just stick to the facts hard as it may be. Write these in pencil not pen. I will explain shortly.

....

....

....

....

....

....

....

....

....

....

....

....

....

....

....

....

....

....

....

....

....

Okay, now that you did the parts you are not grateful for, write in pen this time the things you are thankful for that you see within yourself. It may be that you are easy to talk to and you find it easy to listen to others without judgment which makes others and you feel good. Maybe it's your resilience and how you don't give up on yourself in the tough times. Go for it, write down everything with a pen that you are grateful for about yourself.

Gratitude

....

....

....

....

....

....

....

....

....

....

....

....

....

....

....

....

....

....

If you are like most people, you will have found the first part easier whereby you write the things you are not grateful or appreciative about within yourself. Maybe you knew that instinctively that is how you function. Perhaps this exercise was an eye opener as you get to see what you wrote versus what you thought in your head. Either way, nothing is wrong, and both activities reveal to you more about you to you.

The reason for asking you to write the first one in pencil is because as you start practising gratitude more and more and see the benefits for yourself, you can go back and rub out the things that no longer apply. I acknowledge Lisa Nichols, author and speaker for the idea about writing in pencil and rubbing things out as you progress. Lisa is well known for her transformational work with multi-national businesses and teens. She openly discusses in her interviews how she put her hand on her baby's stomach and vowed to "never be as broke or broken ever again". Lisa lived off welfare and had an abusive partner who was in prison for the majority of her child's life. Today she talks openly about the many areas of her life, mainly gratitude. As a result, she helps others transform their lives.

10 YOU DO NOT SEE WHAT TO BE GRATEFUL FOR IN LIFE

"when you rise in the morning, give thanks for the light, for your life, for your strength. Give thanks for the food and for the joy of living. If you see no reason to give thanks, the fault lies in yourself."
Tecumseh

You may be reading all this as a readout of curiosity, out of intellectual training to learn more. You have read everything so far but done none of the excises, or maybe you have done some of the exercises. Do you feel overwhelmed?. Alternatively, have you told yourself you would do the rest later?. Wherever you are right now in your reading and understanding, it is ok. You are where you are, and that is all it is — nothing more and nothing less.

If you have had a life with very few breaks where every penny counts, it's all been about others, giving and surviving on a pay cheque to pay cheque kind of living, then the next chapter may be of more help to you. It entails being grateful even in the situation you are in at this very moment. As we discussed earlier, it is the lack of gratitude you have for what you have that is creating the poverty. The failure to notice and not just feel but express and act upon and share from that gratitude. As we have discussed throughout this book, there is a direct correlation between appreciation and being enough and having enough. There is also a relationship between gratitude and happiness. It is present to all that you have, rather than what you don't have. Chuck Berry packs no punches and hits straight home with his simple and yet powerful statement. Chuck states that he is grateful every day because we never know when our time is up.

Maybe things are not going right for you, or how you planned or envisioned them. Perhaps you are so focused on the big things and feel that if and when and once accomplished you could and should and would be grateful. However, as we have been saying throughout the whole book gratitude doesn't work like that. It is not about getting what you want, how you want and when you want and then being grateful. It is about being thankful for the present, right now exactly how it is, exactly where it is and where you are standing. I know that is hard to swallow if you are struggling with one thing or many things in your life. I hear you, and feel for you, I do, and

I also know that wallowing in should and could does not work. Gratitude works.

If a man who did not know he would ever make out alive from the Holocaust can make jokes while living off one meal of watery soup and be grateful then surely we can give it a go. As Author, journalist and lecturer A.J Jacobs states he started to look at life from a whole new light. He thanked God for every meal, every sip of water, for waking up. All these little acts of gratitude led him to be more grateful for his whole life and the miracle that he was alive..

Benedictine monk, David Steindl-Rast states that there are two inherent qualities associated with gratitude. The first being appreciation and the second is that gratitude is gratis, i.e. given freely to you.

Robert Emmons in comparison also mentions gratitude having two parts. The first part is "an affirmation of goodness", i.e. you affirm "that there are good things in the world, gifts and benefits we've received". The second part is that "we recognise that the sources of this goodness are outside of ourselves" and "we acknowledge that other people gave us many gifts, big and small, to help us achieve the goodness in our lives". Perhaps this is why you hear Muslims say "those who do not thank people, won't thank God". Much of the research on gratitude shows that although it is a feeling that spontaneously emerges from within us, it is also a choice that requires action. Seeing all that we have you get to be grateful or ungrateful in your choosing.

If you are struggling look at yourself, your body and all that it undergoes, how it is automated and performs without you telling it what to do. Furthermore, look at your family, people around you, the elements, the food you eat, the clothes you wear, the job you have, the car or bike you have. Take a look, particularly at those things that have been given to you free of accord and you enjoy and the benefit. Chapters 7, 11 and 12 below, we discuss the practical ways to express gratitude.

You may have a car, but it is not the car of your dreams or even really that you wanted. However, it gets you from A to B. You may be in a loving relationship but your partner doesn't do the washing up, or the hovering or take the dog out or do the cooking or the DIY but they earn to help you with the food, the mortgage, the kids, the bills and keeping the roof over your head. Things may not be perfect, or according to how you want them, and they never are. So is it not the time to be grateful for what you have right now, and acknowledge the good we do have, so that when we do get more, we can learn to appreciate that too?.

David Steindl-Rast highlights that being grateful in life is the key to a happy life and how we that we hold that in our hands. If we are not thankful, then no matter how much we have we will not be happy because we will always want to have something else or something more.

It is about recognising that life is a gift that was given to you, regardless of how sad, lonely, disappointed, stressed, alone, overwhelmed, negative or empty you may feel. It is about being able to appreciate the gift with all its ups and downs, and it may not be possible to be grateful all the time. It may require you stopping and looking for the goodness, acknowledging it before you move on.

Guri Mehta, an advocate of grateful living, highlights the importance of Living gratefully in a world where we are continually striving for more and better that we lose sight of the all the riches that lay before us and within us. Mehta points out that grateful living is a way of being in life whereby you notice the smallest to the most significant blessings and by doing so take nothing for granted. Instead, you appreciate the present by being present to the abundance there is in nature, such as rain or the number of leaves or fruit on a tree, or the stars at night.

During the more difficult times living a grateful life helps us to be aware of the opportunities for growth and development. As a result, we can reach out to others out of compassion, empathy and kindness.

Is it possible that you have not been seeing what there is to be grateful about because of how you have thus far been relating to gratitude?.

11 GRATITUDE BLOCKERS

"Reflect on your present moment of blessings, of which every man has plenty; not on your past misfortunes of which all men have some."
Charles Dickens

Many people, yes including those who have practised gratitude for years struggle and come across obstacles during their practice. Ralph Waldo Emerson, informs us that "five great enemies to peace inhabit us: avarice, ambition, envy, anger and pride. The chief enemies of gratitude are greed, pride, envy and narcissism. Envy is when your viewing with malice or yearn for what someone else has. As a result, the more we compare ourselves and desire what others have, the more we become dissatisfied with our present circumstances. Therefore, envy creates an illusion of lack and envy feeds into greed. It is then very tempting to hoard (we discuss this later) to compensate for the lack you perceive.

The hubris of arrogance and pride uphold envy and greed. Many religions regard pride as the worst one because it contains the seeds of jealousy, pride, arrogance, anger. Vanity includes an unhealthy amount of self-absorption and superiority so that you see and feel your above other people, other cultures, other religions, the law and so on. This pride feeds further into the self-absorption as you remain in your head, with your thoughts, rather than take action, and yes possibly, fail once or even many times over. It is these emotions, the unexamined goals, wants and ambitions combined with the feelings of defeat and anger at the situation, at people. It creates an air of 'entitlement'. As we talk about later in detail, gratitude and entitlement don't sit well together. Instead, entitlement breeds a lack of appreciation.

In the next chapters, we discuss ways to practice gratitude in further detail. In the meantime, regarding gratitude blockers, it is important first to be aware of the feelings as they arise. Don't fear them or worry that you cannot practice gratitude if they continuously occur. If a young eight years old can write a gratitude journal and express what they are grateful for, there is hope for us, as adults. It is merely a shifting of your perspective to all that what we currently have.

Martin Seligman often referred to as the father of positive psychology states that we can look at life as two-fold, i.e. hold both ideas in our minds at the same time, without one diminishing the other. He encourages us to look at life from the viewpoint of what is working without denying the present situation or circumstances you may be in and thereby cultivate a more positive way of thinking and an attitude of gratitude into our lives. Being realistic and positive about what is working in our lives, we can remind ourselves of how blessed we indeed are. In turn, it helps you to be more thankful and appreciative for all that is working in your life.

Gratitude nurtures you and allows you to create greater purpose in your life. It opens up doors rather than restricts you. It opens you to being freer, provides you with a greater sense of connection to the world and enables you to act out of generosity. Remaining ungrateful will keep you confined, mulling over old fears constricting you as you go round and round a vicious cycle of self-entitlement, combined with envy and greed and desiring what others have. You get to choose.

Co-founder of X-prize, and author, Peter Diamandis has 28 laws that he refers to as "the creed of the passionate and persistent mind". Peter recommends that if you don't have challenges in your life, you should create them. He is not referring to obstacles such as those mentioned above which block gratitude. He appears to be referring to the need to remain challenged, to embrace pain and the struggle in your life rather than become lazy, sit feeling sorry for yourself and watch TV all day.

If there is no resistance in your life, if there is no necessity in your life to do anything, then you will become lazy and will end up pondering why others have what you want. It may lead to feeling envy and greed but without the want to do anything to improve the situation.

Sooner or later, the resignation and resentment will begin to manifest itself, and you will feel them as obstacles in your way. You may look back if you have been that way for a long time, and wonder how did you get to be that way. You are sitting on the comfy, slightly worn couch with a bag of Doritos, last night's pizza, a few cans of extra strong beer. The box of chocolates that you hid from yourself at the very back of the cupboard or on top of the fridge, in case of absolute emergencies, or with a bag of weed, or maybe everything together, all at once. You wait for the take away delivery bike to knock at the door with your chicken wings, extra large pizza, 2 litre bottle of pepsi and garlic bread, and don't forget the cheesy nachos and sticky chocolate pudding for desert.

You wait for the takeaway delivery bike to knock at the door with your chicken wings, an extra large pizza, a 2-litre bottle of Pepsi and garlic bread, and don't forget the cheesy nachos and sticky chocolate pudding for dessert. Where there is no necessity, there is no motivation. How can you be genuinely grateful if everything handed to you?. Yes I know you're arguing with me in your head already, telling me that of course, you would be, what do I know? Right?.

Why are some of the most world's wealthiest people who have everything not happy, not feel great joy and gratitude or skip around everywhere because they have it all? (did I overdo it with the skipping analogy?. Do you think a hopping analogy would have been better?.How about something along the lines of Zebedee or Tigger?. you got what I meant though. Right?). I guess you could say many a movie star, music mogul, pop star or the super wealthy should all be happy just because of all that they have. They appear to have it all, and yet they take drugs, drink excessively, fall into extreme behaviours of all sorts. Many end their lives early either due to unhealthy lifestyles or because they commit suicide.

I know, I know, you are probably wondering why we are talking about all this depressing stuff when the title is about gratitude. That would be a good question. That is because the aim was to highlight how it is not about the money or the amount of 'stuff' you have, rather those very things you are envious of and craving of because others possess them is what is keeping you in the attitude of ingratitude. You are the cause. You are causing the obstacles to appear. You are creating them due to the very nature of how you are perceiving and viewing things around you, i.e. with a lack of gratitude. No matter how hard you try, you cannot be grateful and angry or grateful and sad or grateful and envious, or grateful and full of self-importance at the same time.

Until you change the way you look at what you already have in your life and become grateful, you will always have obstacles. Those obstacles may be in the guise of people, things, money, work, a job, promotion, a pay rise, relationships, or any other resource you are longing after.

Perhaps it is relationships that you are wanting and see others and want what they have. However, all you do is complain and whine, and gossip about women in your life or the men in your life be that at work, at university, at college, in your community, or anywhere else you meet people. You always tell people you want to be in a relationship and how great you are, and yet all you do is complain about how awful the opposite sex is. You are always comparing one person to another, your previous relationship and how awful she/he was, and you tell everyone who will listen. So you then you wonder why you are attracting the same type of relationship and cannot break the cycle. Alternatively, you wonder why things never change for you. They would change if you changed your thinking and started being grateful for those people who are already in your life — also, the people who used to be in your life.

There is a wise saying that states that "some people come into your life for a season, a reason or a lifetime and it is your fault if you confuse them". I can tell you without a shadow of a doubt that I have made that mistake many times in the past. It is once you start being grateful for those that came into your life that you can appreciate what they taught you. The experience may have been positive, or it may be negative. However, you still learnt something. Maybe you learnt how not to be or how to be in your next relationship; more empathetic, communicate more or listen more. I highly recommend reading about the life of Russian playwright, Anton Chekhov who could have focused on lack and his circumstances and become ungrateful. Thankfully he didn't.

If relationships matter to you, I highly recommend Gary Chapman's book "The 5 Languages of Love". According to Gary, there are five love languages; words of affirmation, acts of service, receiving gifts, quality time and physical touch. You may be amazed and finally understand why when you were buying so many expensive gifts for your parent, partner, spouse or friend they didn't appreciate it. Could it be that their love language is acts of service or quality time?. If you want an example of a couple who went on the journey of discovering their love languages, look up, Jay Shetty. Jay, was previously a monk for three years. However, he now thrives as an entrepreneur and coach. There is an excellent video of him and his wife as they openly and honestly talk about getting their love languages so wrong at the beginning.

12 GRATITUDE JOURNAL

"Develop an attitude of gratitude, and give thanks for everything that happens to you, knowing that every step forward is a step toward achieving something bigger and better than your current situation."
Brian Tracy

You may be struggling even as we speak with many issues in your life and want a quick fix to all your problems. Maybe you want to hide or wallow in the past as you look at your present issues and feel they are insurmountable. Well, there is action, and then there is action. The funny thing about decisions is that even deciding not to do something is a decision. It is a choice to be a beneficial or non-beneficial choice. Be happy at least you have been making choices. It is better than life just happening and you not even participating in it.

Are you struggling with people? Great (yes you heard that right, great.) because they are helping you to see parts of you that you cannot see or don't want to tackle. These people may be your friends, co-workers, colleagues, family, maybe even people you rarely see but do see as part of your bigger network. Perhaps you suffer from an anxiety disorder. You may have labelled yourself as shy, uncomfortable, awkward dare I say in public, but you are fine on a one to one basis. Maybe you feel you don't like people, or perhaps it is certain types of people. Ok so if all that or that and more is going on for you, that is great. Yes great. Now that you recognise and acknowledge all that, and you have me admitting it with you, yes you do (smile, don't look so worried. I am with you throughout this whole process. Well someone has to be right, as you keep doubting it all. We all go through this so don't beat yourself up, or hideaway and convince yourself it's not how you feel.)

As the old saying goes "even prophets struggled". Your life in comparison to theirs will look like a breeze. They were either stoned, orphaned, abandoned by their siblings, left for dead, put into a basket to float down the river, underwent constant death threats, ridiculed by their or my own family, had food and water supplies cut off, or accused of being a magician or sorcerer amongst other things.

Often it takes comparing yourself to those who have truly struggled and yet were still successful in seeing what you have. Try it and also try it next time you are struggling. Author John Ortberg said it well "Gratitude is the ability to experience life as a gift. It liberates us from the prison of self pre-occupation".

Someone may have hurt you, done you wrong or your expectations not met in some form or other. You have suffered a significant hardship or hardships that you still are feeling the effects of or unable, maybe even unwilling to forgive and let go. It is during this time that gratitude would be of the most significant benefit. You can allow the hardship to be a blessing because you have allowed it to spur you on, develop and transform yourself.

You could allow the circumstances to continue to increase your resentment, the feelings of self-pity, making others wrong so that you look good and feel good so that you don't have to look at yourself. It may be more comfortable, but as Zen Buddhist monk, Muso Kokushi reiterates what the Quran, Bible, Torah and the many other religions say, i.e. you can let it be a hardship that brings you to ease or become a curse. You get to choose. Now without sounding like Mr Miyagi from the Karate Kid movie, choose wisely.

Goethe said "Know thyself?, if I knew myself, I would run away" and Henry Wadsworth Longfellow said, " if we could read the secret history of our enemies, we should find in each man's life sorrow and suffering enough to disarm all hostility."

Before we move on what I am trying to get to here is, is to look at how we all view things. Is it possible, that it is not what has happened that is disturbing you? Instead as Epictetus states, the view you are taking of the events or incident that occurred?. Maybe none of this making any sense, perhaps you are reading it, but you don't want it to make sense because then you may have to scratch beneath the surface, look inside and stop pointing fingers at others. Maybe, maybe you are fearful if you are grateful, it means that you have enough and you will stop striving. You may feel like you don't want to transform your life by being grateful or perhaps you do but on your terms and only a little. That's great. Yes great because as Socrates said, "the secret of change is to focus all of your energy, not on fighting the old, but building the new".

It may be that the reason(s) you don't feel grateful is because you have been focusing all your energy simultaneously on living in and yet fighting the past. In essence that which won't change no matter how hard anyone tries or wills it. True forgiveness is being able to look at what has happened and saying "thank you for that experience" by seeing the positive in it. Be honest, is there anything holding you back?. Do you think if I had more money, a new car, or that partner, a particular incident hadn't happened, you had taken that job, not accepted that job, married that person, not married that person, not made that loan, not lent that money, that had not happened or that had happened, then you would have been grateful?. In the space below write down what is stopping you being genuinely appreciative. Maybe you don't see how you act or behave when you are ungrateful. If you can't then ask someone around you to see your blind spots and point them out.

....

....

....

....

....

....

....

....

....

Ok let us look at what you can do practically to help get you out of your head, so this is not just another nice concept and brain exercise that you forget. I know many of us will think like that because having asked people it was clear that people did not understand or practice gratitude. Some people due to their faith knew about gratitude and exercised it while the majority viewed it as something nice to do. I get it; I do because for the longest time it felt like a concept for me too, a theory, something nice to mull over. You and I both know though that there is no power or aliveness or life in a concept. Gratitude requires practice daily for it to be grasped and understood on a more profound and yet more fundamental level.

The question of inner and outer gratitude will, and needs to become one. What is the point of being, feeling grateful towards people and not saying it?. There is no benefit because as Gertrude Stein said: "Silent gratitude isn't of any use to anyone". Gratitude needs expressing out aloud because it benefits both the receiver and the giver. Feeling grateful and not expressing William Arthur Ward described it as "a bit like wrapping a present and not giving it".

John F. Kennedy also mentioned there being great merits in expressing gratitude and encouraged people by highlighting that "You need to make time and thank people who have helped you, made a difference in your life".

Before you start groaning, dismissing the very thought, rolling your eyes, merely reading over this or kissing your teeth (yes I know about that one), mentioning you don't have the time or if you should, could, would, what would mother say? Alternatively, what would the neighbours say?; let's leave them out of it for now. Ok now that we have pre-empted your excuses, oops, I mean reasons, let's start taking some action. It is easy, start with something small, even the laziest person could do some of these actions. Ready?, nod your head in agreement and say yes loudly (think Rocky with Sylvester Stallone, kind of yes). Did you nod your head? Yes? Good. If you did not go ahead and nod. Ok, good. I don't want to be the only one doing all the work here. Remember this is a partnership. Once I have completed this book I may apply to work in the Marine Corps, Navy or the Army; I want to be able to say, "am I clear solider?. what do you think? (don't laugh..... I am sharing).

Choose a notebook and a nice pen. Maybe get a diary as it has all the dates in already. If you are starting now and it is not 1st of January you might be better off with the notebook. If you are home, then find a notebook, preferably a thick one that will last for a year. It does not matter if it doesn't but something with several hundred pages, so there is some consistency. At the top of the page in your new notebook put the date. See I told you even the laziest person could do this. If you are at work, then pop out in your lunch break or on the way home and buy one from the stationary store. No, don't just go and take one from the stationary cupboard at work. The notebook is for personal use so let's not in essence 'steal' from work and start on the wrong foot. If you do have a habit of taking or so-called 'borrowing' stuff from work and not returning it, you are saying that you cannot afford to buy it yourself. You probably can purchase it if you are honest but choose to justify it and remain unaware of what you have or are ungrateful or maybe both.

You may not like what I said. You may not see it as anything of significance or may even completely ignore it. Naturally, the choice is yours, but it is a big thing because if that is what you do out of habit then really what you are saying, particularly to yourself, perhaps without even realising, is that you don't have enough; therefore you need to steal. In comparison, a grateful heart is content and focuses on what you do have, not on what you don't have. Maybe you have a minimal budget each month, and it barely stretches to the end of the month. So spending on non-essentials such as a notebook for yourself is seen as a luxury, not a necessity and therefore a waste of money. Ok, let's work with what you have, you could purchase a cheaper, less fancy notebook from the dollar or pound store or the local supermarket where they sell items for school children so notebooks may be more affordable.

There honestly was a reason for sharing that. It is easy to take for granted how so many people can go into a shop and pretty much buy anything they want to eat, drink or possibly use or wear. On the flip side, not everyone has that luxury and I know or have met or worked with people that you genuinely would think that there is no way they struggle with money or have any issues in life. Imagine my surprise when I have got to know the individual, and they share how much they are fighting, and their life is hanging by a thread. The clothes they are wearing may look fancy and expensive but are from the local thrift/charity store, and the reason they don't claim to have had a big breakfast is that that way no one will ask about lunch. They never go out in the evenings with the rest of the team because they cannot afford to and are fearful if they have to chip in extra or pay a tip. It may then mean having to find extra money to then pay for the rent.

I am aware though it can be vice versa whereby someone wealthy doesn't dress like a millionaire. The first time I met someone like that and my line manager told me how much the man in the big woolly coat that had come into the investment bank was worth I almost fell out of my chair and banged my head on the way down. To say I was surprised would be an understatement. It would be a case of eating several of my hats. There was absolutely nothing saying how this regular looking man was, not that

I expected a sticker on his head, but I did envision at least an Armani overcoat, maybe, rather than the thick woolly coat he donned. I know I mentioned investment banking in there. Don't go thinking that means I am some hedge fund manager or work for Warren Buffett or caused the financial collapse. It was a temporary role and not even as a banker, and if you don't believe me, you can ask my old manager Steve, the banker, who wore braces with his suit, or was that Al Capone?.

Ok now that we have lightened the atmosphere. It was getting a bit heavy wasn't it, but it needed to be said and done because we all struggle with certain areas in life.

So instead of feeling you have to buy a notebook, or take from your workplace, you could just cut an A4 piece of paper into small squares. We will talk about that in a moment, for now back to the gratitude journal.

Open your journal, write in today's date at the top, yes today's date. No time like the present and commence writing at least 15 things you are grateful for that have happened today. If it is early morning, afternoon or evening it's okay. I would highly recommend as do many advocates of the gratitude journal that you do this at the start of the day before you go about the day. The morning is said to be more effective and recommended because the world is quiet and your mind is calm and has space to think before the busyness of the day. While in the evening, you can then reflect on all the good things that happened throughout the day before you go to sleep. Some days you may see or receive more, and that's ok too. Maybe someone offered you a seat on a busy train, tube or bus, write that down. Then write down why you are grateful, for example, offered a seat meant you could sit and drink your morning coffee and put your heavy rucksack on the floor under your chair. You may have been grateful because you weren't having a good morning and the very fact that someone showed you kindness made your day, and you instantly felt better and had a great day. If that was the case, write that down. I remember travelling recently on a busy, noisy morning train with people being rude or arguing with someone on their mobile phone when I wanted to close my eyes and sleep for the duration of the ride. I then rushed onto a bus which passed by Regents Park when I happened to look up and saw the BT telecom tower said: "Good Morning London" in letters going round at the top of it. I smiled and was thankful how although the people on the train were so loud and angry at least the tower was polite and friendly as it illuminated "good morning" pleasantly in bright colours.

Some days you may feel there is nothing to be grateful for but you know that's not true. It may be something simple as someone held a door open for you, or someone smiled at you. Appreciate it for what it is, someone saw you and kept the door open out of kindness; someone smiled out of compassion. Write it down and don't take it for granted. Learn to notice the goodness and be thankful because a sense of gratitude and feeling blessed comes from the heart, not from more blessings. If you really cannot think of anything to be grateful then focus on the simple fact that you woke up alive or for your breath.

If you always walk the same route to work, sit with the same people, at the same desk, go to the same shops then mix it up a bit. Sit with different people, hotdesk in another area, go to a different shop on your way to work or home, walk through the park, read an alternative newspaper, read a different genre in books, or magazines, watch a different movie. What was it that Einstein said about insanity, exactly, doing the same thing and expecting a different result. I am not saying you're insane. I am, however, suggesting you do some different things to help you see and awaken your senses because the eyes and mind and ears are suitably bored of seeing and looking and hearing the same every day that it has become a routine that you don't notice the good even when it is there. Once you start seeing all the goodness surrounding you and feeling grateful, you will find that you can write more than 15 things to be thankful each day. It just takes a little practice.

Please don't make it into this huge thing so that you feel like not even starting. If writing what you are grateful for each evening seems enough then start with that. You can then work towards saying why you are thankful for each of the things that occurred, or you saw, heard or felt during the day.

If you are in any doubt about the benefits of journaling, ask TV host, philanthropist and billionaire Oprah Winfrey who has admitted to keeping a gratitude journal since her 20's. I can vouch for that the very practice of putting pen to paper has helped immensely to create awareness, get out of my head and acknowledge the goodness in my life. Like all of us, the focus had been on what we don't have rather than what we do. There was a time in my life when I didn't write a gratitude journal and then took it up followed by dropping it for almost a year. I can tell you I most definitely noticed the impact, and it was not a good one. I got back into old habits as we all do. (I know, I know, that little voice in your head is off, and you have started the judgement. Am I right or am I right? It's ok. His wife has told even gratitude researcher, Robert Emmons who has been researching gratitude for over a decade that he is the most ungrateful person. As a result, he too undertakes practical gratitude exercises to enable and remind him to be grateful. See there is hope.)

I am thankful that happened because it has helped me to see the benefits and the power in writing things down. It also enabled me to see how much we miss throughout the day and walk around with our eyes closed. However, if you know, you are going to be writing in your gratitude journal you are suddenly more aware and notice things to appreciate. As a result, you see more.

Vishen Lakhani, (author of 'The Code of the Extraordinary Mind') interviewed Robin Sharma (author of 'The Monk Who Sold His Ferrari ' and 'the 5 AM Club') whereby Robin talks about gratitude and how it really saved him and helped build his life more than 20 years ago. Furthermore Robin discussed how the brain is hardwired for negativity, and we all have what psychologists call, and he referred to as a 'negative bias', and as a result, gratitude acts as an "antidote". He highlighted how the practice of physically practising gratitude creates new neurological pathways in the brain leading to greater clarity. Furthermore, research has found that people watching the news, rather than having a better view of reality, see less of reality.

Robin beautifully illustrates how writing a gratitude journal is not about a set of rules and one way and only one way to do it. He shows you during the interview how to have fun with it, as he talks about how and what he writes. It is more free-flowing whereby sometimes Robin wrote his top 25 "I am grateful............", other times pours out his pain or writing lists of what wants to accomplish combined with pictures and cut-outs of his desires. He emphasises the importance of consistency and how gratitude truly changed his life to a more fulfilling one although he was successful before and on the road to becoming a judge, earning a high salary, but felt unhappy and unfulfilled regardless of all that he had accumulated.

Robin echoes in his interview what French writer, historian and philosopher Voltaire said, i.e. "when the evening began, Fouquet was at the top of the world. By the time it had ended, he was at the bottom". Robin highlights how your habits and how your happiness is dependent on what you do every day, i.e. your habits. It takes 66 days to install a practice before it becomes automatic and enables you.

It is an excellent interview, relaxed, filled with many insights, that come at you thick and fast. Thankfully, Vishen recaps it all at the end of the conversation.

On a side note to those of you who have asked about writing by hand with pen and paper logging things on your phone; I cannot recommend enough that you write with pen and paper. Yes, I appreciate we are still writing regardless of be it a pen touching paper or on your phone. However, there is a difference, a different feeling when you are typing it out into your phone than when you are writing it using a pen. It is not about the right or wrong way. There is power in the written word, and something is satisfying sitting and writing it out using a pen and paper. Give it a try, and if you absolutely cannot then try the phone. At least consider it for six months using pen and paper. Hey, write in and let me know how it goes.

Ok, let's commit to doing this. You can do this (look at me sounding like a sports coach and a well-known sports shoe advert). On the space on the next page write down in pen, today's date, and then copy onto the dotted lines what's written below the line.

....
(today's date)

....

....
I commit that starting today (add today's date) to write

....

....
in my new gratitude journal what I am grateful for each day

....
add your signature above

13 WHY GRATITUDE IS GOOD FOR YOU

"Gratitude unlocks the fullness of life. It turns what we have into enough and more. It turns denial into acceptance, chaos into order and confusion into clarity. It turns problems into gifts, failures into success, the unexpected into perfect timing, and mistakes into important events. Gratitude makes sense of our past, brings peace for today and creates a vision for tomorrow."
Melody Beattie

Dr Norman Rosenthal, psychiatrist and author of "Winter Blues," highlights that gratitude may not come naturally to some people; however, it can be learnt and cultivated into a habit.

Eammons author and professor of psychology undertook research that showed a surprising number of health benefits. Gratitude showed to decrease blood pressure, improve the immune system, enabling better sleep, improved moods, less fatigued. Another study undertaken at the University of California showed that grateful people had improved heart health, notably better heart rhythms and less inflammation.

Research conducted at the universities of Kentucky and Utah found that positive law students had higher levels of disease-fighting cells in their bodies. Similar results have shown with older people If they were worried about getting dementia or Alzheimer's compared to those who were positive about their future. Eammons research showed that people who kept a gratitude journal had a reduced fat intake, almost 25% lower. Besides stress hormones in those who were grateful were 23% lower.

Furthermore, research highlighted that the daily practice of gratitude could well reduce the effects of ageing particularly on the brain. Emmons states that the impact of gratitude may well be due to the feelings that felt as a result of feeling grateful.

Developing gratitude leads to healthier, stronger relationships because grateful people tend to appreciate others more and show their appreciation. In effect, it is a cyclical reinforcing pattern. Grateful people are happier, sleep better, enjoy better relationships and have a tendency to look after themselves, making better health choices and therefore tend to be healthier.

Researchers from the University of Indiana studied a group of 43 people suffering from anxiety or depression.

Half of the group wrote thank you letters to people they knew. All 43 individuals undertook an MRI scan while told someone had given them a lump sum of money and if they would like to donate to charity out of gratitude. The MRI scan showed particular brain activity from those who gave money. Those who had undertaken the writing of thank you letters reported feeling more gratitude two weeks after the exercise than those who had not written gratitude letters. Besides, those who wrote the thank you letters to people in their lives expressing gratitude showed further gratitude related brain activity months later under an MRI scan.

The brain is like a muscle. The more you practice, the more you strengthen it and the easier it becomes to be grateful. The more you allow yourself to recognise and then acknowledge everything that you can be and are thankful for, the more your brain will adapt to that way of thinking. Once you start practising it, you will notice you more and feel higher levels of gratitude. It is instead like when you buy a brand new red car. You suddenly start seeing all the other red cars on the road. They were there before, but you never saw them. They were not in your awareness, so you did not acknowledge them. Gratitude works similarly, now that you are focusing on it, you will notice far more things to be appreciated.

14 PRACTICAL TIPS

"Develop an attitude of gratitude. Say "thank you" to everyone you meet for everything they do for you."
Brian Tracy

In the previous chapter, we spoke about the gratitude journal in detail. Below are other practical ways to practice gratitude. Mainly for all of you who wanted to know how to express gratitude. Pick and choose what works for you. You may do one thing and stick to that and be a champion at that, or you may do a couple of things and create that as a new habit. Eammons research showed the dominant effects on the participants had after undertaking the gratitude journaling. Furthermore, research shows that writing about what you are grateful each day for two weeks has a profoundly positive impact that lasts up to 6 months later.

Gratitude Jar

I mentioned this above in the gratitude journal chapter as another option for those struggling to buy a journal. You may want to try this with young children who may struggle with writing a journal every day. Make it fun with different coloured pens and possibly stickers or drawings for them.

Take an A4 piece of paper and cut it into small squares and each day write all the things you appreciate. You can write five on each piece of paper. The number is not essential because you want to jot down as many as possible. I recommended earlier at least 15 when writing the gratitude journal. My disclaimer is that this should be fun so you may start with 10 and build your way up. It is far more vital that you start doing this today. Involve the partner, the children, the housemates, the flatmates to do this too.

Pebble

You may want to keep a stone in your pocket, or a semi-precious stone like jade so that each time you touch it, you are reminded to be grateful. I did not find this helpful as I would lose the stone or forget to carry it with me. I also felt I would prefer to say "thank you" naturally; however, you can try it, it may work for you.

Bracelet/Necklace

Each time you touch a bead on the bracelet you are reminded to be grateful. It may be easier for many people because you are firstly wearing it on your wrist or around your neck. Many Muslims, Jews, Christians, and

Buddhists practice gratitude using rosary beads. There are a specific number of beads on the necklace/bracelet, and as each one is touched a prayer of gratitude is said audibly. It is also a form of meditation and a way to relax and focus the mind on all that you are grateful for to God.

Say thank you

Thank you card and Thank you letters and emails
Studies show the power of these small actions. Participants were asked in one study to send an email to someone explaining their gratitude to the other person who had powerfully impacted their lives. Those who wrote the emails had not estimated the response from the receiver who was touched, moved and surprised. The receivers saw the writers as warm and capable, not something the writers had thought or expected as an outcome of their letters. It reiterates the work undertaken in 2007 by Robert Emmons. Eammons looked at gratitude on a deeper level and how it affected people and found that expressing gratitude improves mental, physical, emotional and relational wellbeing.

At the dinner table routine

There are so many people I would love to have as guests around my dinner table. Yes, my table is small and as the old saying goes, rather than complaining about the number of people get a bigger table. It is not about inviting guests in that sense before I get carried away and list all the people I would want around, that's another book in and of itself. It is more about what Brene Brown, author, social researcher and speaker on Ted talks. Brown talks about feeling joy and feeling vulnerability "we're trying to beat vulnerability to the punch. We don't want to be blind sighted by hurt. We don't want to get caught off guard, so we practice being devastated or never move from self-elected disappointment".

In reality, you are regularly "rehearsing tragedy" and thereby always be living from the worst case scenario, so you're always living in fear and superstition and worried if things go good your tempting the fates. Maybe it is easier to live "disappointed than it is to feel disappointed...............you sacrifice joy, but you suffer less."

Brown reiterates that allowing ourselves to feel joy requires vulnerability and it may not feel natural, and you may have an emotional and even a physical reaction to being vulnerable. Brown admits herself to struggling with it herself. She talks about how those who "rehearse tragedy" don't allow all the pictures that come up when they feel the joy to take hold in their mind as they feel overwhelmed with joy. It is the fear of the unknown; it means taking a risk, allowing yourself to stand with the possibility of being uncertain and open about how you respond to joy because as Brown says "we are desperate for more joy, but at the same time we can't tolerate the vulnerability". It is then, and the most critical time to express your gratitude, as you feel the overwhelm, as you become uncertain, as you start having an emotional and physical reaction and don't want to think or feel or look vulnerable. Feeling joy is a perfect gift and time to express your gratitude.

Brown's research over 12 years highlighted that the magic pill (I knew to watch The Matrix would come in handy one day. Oh. Those of you who are rolling your eyes, don't worry you can change it to antidote as per Marvel movies, Spiderman, Incredible Hulk, X Men). Ok now that we have satisfied every movie buff, back to the subject of what the "antidote" is when you are feeling vulnerable while you're experiencing those moments of joy is, yes you guessed it, gratitude.

Now that we have discussed vulnerability and how it's linked to gratitude lets come back to the dinner table. The dinner table routine is about creating a habit of asking each other at the dinner table what you are grateful for during that day you experienced. You may find that no one has much to say on the first day. Keep going because as you keep practising a breakthrough will occur, and you will be amazed at people opening up of their own accord about what they noticed that day and felt appreciation. You may find you're repeating or others are repeating what they are thankful for, that is ok, allow them to do that because maybe that is all they can see. I recently asked a couple of young children what they were grateful for and was surprised to hear they couldn't think of anything. Rather than admonish them, I suggested a few things such as their eyes, the ability to breathe to start them off. Once they got the idea, they came up with many things themselves. Sometimes it takes a little help, even as adults.

Food

There is a Japanese phrase 'itadakimsu', which is said before eating, i.e. 'thank you for the food'. The eater is thanking the farmer for growing the food, the nourishment it provides and those who cooked it.

Many religions also encourage you to say thanks to God for the food before eating. Another way to show your appreciation for the food you eat is to do so mindfully. It is about being fully present to what you are eating without watching TV or playing on a mobile device or eating as quickly as possible while walking to work. It is about eating without distraction and enjoying the meal to its fullest.

The Fridge

Not my idea, although naturally, I wish it had been, I recently heard an interview but at this very moment do not recall who it was, although I seem to remember Lewis Howes (former professional football player, author and entrepreneur) interviewing or was it Tom Bilyeu (entrepreneur and co-founder of Quest Nutrition). I know it wasn't Vishen Lakhiani who interviewed Robin Sharma, whom we discussed earlier. The suggestion was to stick pictures of people that you are grateful for in your life. I felt I had to include this because it is such a simple act and yet it reminds you not to take people in your life or those you meet for granted.

Prayer

All the major religions have prayers of gratitude. If you practice a particular faith, you can use those prayers of gratitude to enhance your morning routine. Focusing on gratitude is a great way to bring clarity to enable you to start your day and before it gets busy and your attention is needed elsewhere.

If you do not follow a particular faith, you can regardless pray or meditate and express gratitude by giving thanks. In essence, you are acknowledging that the goodness you are receiving is outside of yourself and giving thanks.

Meditation

Each day in the morning, during your lunch break or in the evening you could choose to sit and practice mindful meditation. Allow yourself to sit quietly and focus on all your senses. Close your eyes, breathe deeply from your nose and push the breath down to your stomach feeling it rise and fall a few times. Allow your regular breathing pattern to return as you relax. Bring your awareness to your breath in the present moment. Listen to it and feel it moving throughout your body and feel the feeling of gratitude as your body is being breathed.

Gently allow your awareness to move from your breathing to your sense of smell and as you breathe in and smell, acknowledge the ability to smell and bring your gratitude to that. If you can detect a pleasant scent being thankful.

Now let your awareness drift to your hearing and acknowledge your ability to hear, the ability to distinguish between the different sounds and tones and the ability to recognise them. Maybe you can listen to your breathing. Relax and allow yourself to notice everything around you, don't judge the sounds, let yourself to be in the moment; are they close or far, are there any sounds intermingled, is one sound clearer or do they all merge. Let all the sounds occur. Maybe you can hear your heart beating, the rain or the wind outside. Perhaps you can hear yourself breathing and others breathing around you. Allow yourself to smile if you feel and want to while you sit.

Now allow yourself to move your focus into your eyesight. Keep breathing through the nose while sitting up straight or lying down on your back. Bring your awareness to your eyes and the sensation of the eyeballs in the eye sockets. Are they moist or irritated and gritty or dry? Are they still or racing under the eyelids? Are they sore? Allow yourself to think of all the things your able to see and have seen with your eyes throughout your life. While you are focusing on all the items and places and people your eyes have seen and your ability to be able to see express your gratitude. Then show your appreciation outwardly. It should be audible rather than loud. You may choose to smile and say "thank you", or you may say "thank you for my eyesight and the ability to see all the beauty around me, the ability to see my family and friends".

Allow your awareness to move to your hands as you continue breathing through the nose and allow your breath to move around your body to the areas where you may feel the tension. Allow your breath to nourish you.

Bring your attention to your hands, eyes still closed, move your fingers one by one, touch the palms of your hands, gently rub your hands together and feel the warm generated. Allow your hands to stop moving and place them on your heart, right followed by left. Allow yourself to think of your ability to touch, the ability to feel and how you can feel different textures, the warmth and cold.

Allow yourself to voice your gratitude outwardly. It should be audible but not loud. Let your awareness move to taste by moving your tongue inside your mouth for a moment. Draw into your awareness the different types of tastes and flavours and how you can distinguish those; the salty, the sweet, the sour......and voice your gratitude.

You may wish to end your mindful meditation there with a simple opening of the eyes and a thank you, or you may want to continue depending on how you feel. Most people prefer 5-10 minutes and feel that is enough to help them reconnect to themselves, particularly when things get busy. It is a simple tool because gratitude is not just in our heads because as a researcher, speaker and author Joe Dispenza said if it were, everyone would be happy. It comes from and is rooted in the heart.

Calendar

Another tip which everyone can join in that you live with or even at work. You could stick the calendar up in the kitchen at home and work. Let others contribute and share your ideas. Write down what you are going to do to express your gratitude each month. Start with one thing a month and make that count before you add more. Start today, don't wait for the next month to start or this month to end. You could express your gratitude this month by cooking for someone you know is always struggling with time for themselves, perhaps you could invite them to dinner on the weekend to show you appreciate them.

You may want to volunteer your time on the weekend to a homeless shelter or animal shelter, help those less fortunate than you are. There does not need to be a grand plan. Starting with something small before working your way up may be more comfortable and more effective. Maybe your good at Maths or IT and you know someone or several people who struggle and would value your help. Perhaps you could volunteer your time by visiting a care home or hospital and read to the patients there. Often in the libraries and local newspapers, there are events, charities, groups and organisations looking for help. It may be as simple as helping pick up litter after a football match or along a canal or river. It really could be anything that entails you giving to others from the recognition of what you've received. Perhaps you're inspired, and you could use your holidays either by yourself, with the whole family, or a group of friends, as a couple or small community to travel abroad and help.

There are so many opportunities and so many people wanting your help that you honestly really don't have to look that far. A quick internet search will reveal a plethora of opportunities near you or abroad.

15 GIVING OUT OF GRATITUDE

"The unthankful heart discovers no mercies, but the thankful heart will find, in every hour, some heavenly blessings."
Henry Ward Beecher

William Ury, co-author of "Getting To Yes" highlighted in his book how the matter of our external view of life lay with the picture we had of it internally. It is by changing the internal that the external will change and not the other way round. Ury adds that if we want to change our position from one of opposition to one of collaboration, then we need "think, act and conduct our relationships as if the universe is essentially a friendly place and life, is in fact on our side".

Ury echoes the words of wise men, philosophers, leaders throughout history and modern-day coaches and philanthropists, that is, "being happy comes from being grateful for life". The opposite would be a life lived, and a mindset focused on scarcity where it is never enough. It is the lack of gratitude and attachment that often leads to aggression, concentrate on the I rather than we, causes stress and anxiety as you push and try to control the situation, all in the name of obtaining more.

The scarcity focused mindset is one of the attachments, lack of flexibility and lack of clarity. It is sticking so tightly to one view and discarding all other possibilities because you want what you want and that causes chaos and misery and lack of gratitude.

Often when we get what we wanted we move on quickly to wanting the next 'new' thing. So many of the things we are attached to cause us difficulties or even pain, but we are still unwilling to let go of them. Therefore the very act of generosity is crucial because it allows breaking the pattern and creates a give and take.

The human mind is particularly fond of grabbing and holding on to any number of things including resources such as wealth, people and possessions. The act of sharing and giving out of generosity encourages the mind to see the world from the frame of enough, and because you view the world from what you have rather than what you don't have, you can give and share.

Giving allows you to free yourself from being attached to things and your self. It may take practice if it does not come naturally for you because as Frank a Clark said:

"We're all generous, but with different things, like time, money, talent - criticism.". It may well be that you don't struggle to give your time but are less than generous with your wealth or talent, or you may be generous with your wealth and yet withhold from sharing the expertise that may be of more significant benefit to those around you.

Practical giving replaces the emotions of loneliness, feeling separated and scarcity. Real giving lends itself to self-liberation by its very nature as it grows out of kindness and concern for others rather than wanting to look good with grand gestures of giving.

Fear and focus on scarcity closes the heart, often leading to greed, jealousy, stinginess and envy combined with a mind that is not at peace as it focuses on 'if's', 'buts' and reasoning the happiness that could have obtained "if only I had more of ...."

Gratitude allows you to meet life where it is. Appreciation will enable you to open your heart and access the wonder of life in the present moment. Practising gratitude frees you while allowing you to reconnect with yourself and the rest of humanity and to life itself. It can soften the heart that has become so focused on the array of dissatisfactions. Practising gratitude doesn't mean there are no longer difficulties; the focus has changed and instead of allowing the mind to become depleted with frustrations and anxieties it can focus on the power of gratitude.

Gratitude is all about the heart. When you naturally grateful you will feel an intense appreciation within your heart. It is out of this sheer appreciation that arises the natural want to be kind, give, share and help others by being generous as others have been towards you.

There is an excellent story in Chris Guillebeau's book "The Happiness of Pursuit" of a traveller who was amazed by the generosity of people as he travelled the world. He got lost so many times, travelled through dangerous parts of the world, ran out of money. Each time he was saved by the kindness of a stranger and said that throughout his journey he kept learning the same lesson again and again "people everywhere are the same". He came to appreciate all the similarities of all the people that most parents love their children and most people want to be happy in their way and enjoyed each country for what it was rather than compare them all and their differences.

To gain more clarity, the art of giving is an essential practice. The heart that focuses on giving reduces the likelihood of the brain deceived by the illusion of attachment. Adam Grant organisational psychologist and professor at Wharton discusses in his book "Give and Take" the importance of giving, the different types of givers (i.e. matchers and takers versus otherish givers and selfish givers), how to avoid burnout and the benefits of giving for yourself too.

Furthermore Adam discusses a 2 year study of firefighters who started to burnout whereby their performance levels decreased as they became less concerned about work, however, the area where they gave more during the same time was in helping their fellow workers with their work, share knowledge, provide a listening ear to those struggling, provide advice to new staff. Grant highlights how the firefighters knew instinctively that by giving they would not only strengthen but also create support.

Giving is said to energise you; however, it is not any old type of offering that does so, i.e. if you feel obliged or forced to it does not to provide you with that energising effect. People had felt a sense of meaning and joy when they helped others out of "enjoyment and purpose" as a result the givers "experienced significant increases in energy ....a greater sense of autonomy, mastery, and connection to others, and it boosted their energy."

Research has shown that giving can significantly raise your levels of happiness. Giving also helps boost your mood and levels of self-esteem as you help other people. Help may be in the form of money or time amongst other resources. Grant highlights how giving gives us meaning in life, as we focus on others, rather than our problems, which further studies have shown in return benefit us.

David Meltzer, one of six children raised by a single mother is interviewed in detail by Tom Bilyeu (Co-founder of Quest Nutrition) how much shame he felt from confronting his mum having failed. He confesses that all he wanted to do was buy his mum a house and car and thought had failed himself and her when he became broke and they repossessed her home. Having lost millions, David made it back and learnt many critical lessons which are openly spoken about with Tom during the interview. He is now an entrepreneur and philanthropist who shares his work on how to be successful in two very successful books 'connected to success' and compassionate capitalism.

One of David's four principles is finding ways to serve others. As a result, whatever he and his business partner Warren Moon do has a charitable element to it. This one simple rule has genuinely increased the growth of their business more so than ever before.

David admits he used to see things as merely a transaction, even giving, whereby he would "give with the expectation of the least appreciation" and adds how it caused many issues. He hit rock bottom, and his attitude changed rock bottom to one of faith and believing if he "was of service and did well and does the right things, true purpose, fulfilment and wealth come to him more accurately and reduces the resistance in his life".

At his highest point, his wife was not happy and told him so. She asked him to take stock of his life because the expensive cars and all the wealth that surrounded them was not cutting it. She was not happy with him and whom he had become. He had lost his core values.

David talks about the four values his mum had taught him. The first one he mentions is gratitude and how although they had nothing, he was a grateful child. Suddenly as an adult his past present and future all looked unpromising.

David expressed how he lost his perspective on gratitude and started blaming and shaming and not taking accountability for his life. In his sharing, he beautifully illustrates how there is no gratitude when you feel entitled. Brene Brown adds that "what separates privilege from entitlement, is gratitude". I highly recommend if you have not already seen the interview online, to do so. Even if you watch the first 10 minutes, you will learn so much about the power of giving and gratitude from a man who came from nothing.

Hey, while you are at it, watch and be inspired by Tom Bilyeu and his wife Lisa known as the billion dollar power couple. He came from humble beginnings while Lisa was accustomed to wealth. Her father like Tom worked hard to from the onset. I will let Omar their interviewer entertain you as they discuss the couple share their stories.

16 HOARDING AND MINIMALISM

"I was complaining that I had no shoes until I met a man who had no feet"
Confucius

Hoarding

Marie Kondo, the Japanese wonder woman of declutter states regarding gratitude "having gratitude for the things your discarding. By giving gratitude, your giving closure to the relationship with that object, and by doing so, it becomes a lot easier to let go."

Research has highlighted the correlation between mental wellbeing and hoarding. The TV programmes reiterate that with many hoarders suffering from mental health issues. It is unclear if there was an underlying tendency in these individuals and the condition became worse once they started to hoard or did the hoarding cause the worsening of their mental health and overall wellbeing. Regardless, the inability to let go often seeped into other areas of their lives. Often the hoarding of items which may be junk to many but precious to many hoarders was as a result of an occurrence or trauma in their lives.

Ryan Nicodemus and Joshua Fields Millburn are the minimalists who gave up very successful corporate jobs in America. We discuss their work below in the chapter about minimalism. The minimalists explain hoarding about DVD collections and how they had thousands of dollars worth of films collecting dust. They ask the question which many of us will have asked " how many times will I watch this movie", it may be your favourite movie but realistically since you purchased your collection how many times have you watched it?. This may be similar to the bag collection, the wardrobe full of clothes that are similar, if you are sincere, because if you love shopping and collecting (another word, albeit it a more beautiful word than hoarding) you will have forgotten you have a similar or that same pair of trousers or dress at home. Maybe your hoard is watches, trainers, ties, shoes, aftershaves and perfumes, utensils, cookware, books, magazines, toys, teddy bears, make-up and the list goes on. Hoarding comes in many guises.

Ryan and Joshua draw our attention to how organising our 'collections' are still hoarding, i.e. "organising is nothing more than well-planned hoarding". It is just a different way of managing all the stuff you have. You then have to clean, maintain and operate all this stuff which in turn causes you to worry, waste time and in essence brings little or no value to your life. You may be quite smart about your organising by vacuum packing your stuff or store things neatly in boxes marked in the garage in addition to hiring space/container as well as saving at your parents home or friends home.

Would it not be more beneficial to spend that time with friends, family, doing something you enjoy rather than organising your stuff and avoiding life and what is truly important?.

Minimalism

You would think they are brothers, but surprisingly they are not. Ryan Nicodemus and Joshua Fields Millburn are the minimalists and travel particularly in America have given up on their wealthy corporate life to lead a more minimalistic lifestyle. It has led them to greater joy, and they have come to be grateful for what they had and realised how consumed both were by consumerism and their "stuff" as they like to call it. So what has gratitude got to do with minimalism you may ask. Good question. Also, rather than explaining the ins and outs of minimalism I wholeheartedly and genuinely recommend looking up the www.theminimalists.com. They actively promote minimalism and have released a documentary aptly called 'Minimalism', podcasts, opened a coffee house, generously donate to those less fortunate, both are speakers to multi-million dollar firms also have a book titled, yes you guessed it "Minimalism".

Also try to read "Goodbye Things" by the Japanese author, Funion Sasaki who has written about his experiences of decluttering and living as a minimalist. Similar to Ryan and Joshua, Saski discovers the freedom from letting things go. All three minimalists share how experiences and connection with those around them became more enjoyable and more in-depth. They became more fulfilled as they let go of their 'stuff'. Letting go of 'stuff' helped them be less overwhelmed, less stressed, and less lonely. They took back control of their lives, became more grateful and more fulfilled. Naturally there are many other blogs, YouTube videos; however, I found the minimalists and the author mentioned above helpful.

The minimalists and Kondo highlight what Eammons and research since then have highlighted which is, the numerous effects of gratitude. In essence, all three men got rid of all the clutter and unnecessary stuff in their lives which freed up space physically and emotionally as they focused less on accumulating more things they didn't need and began appreciating what they had. Besides, they had more time and were willing to spend time with people rather than spending time buying more musical instruments and DVDs and CDs that added to the collection which were collecting dust and yet to unplayed or watched. As time was no longer needed to clean and maintain and worry and spend on goods more time with people and connecting and boosting levels of appreciation and energy and wellbeing.

You will notice this for yourself when you clean up an area where you live; you feel much better afterwards. These three guys did that on a significant scale.

Ask people you know and get to know "how do you see me limiting myself"?. Write down it down and develop an action plan. Remember to thank people; "thank you for caring enough and taking the time to tell me what you see, and how you feel. I am grateful for your insights."

Recognise that there are two stages of gratitude. You are firstly recognising all that is good in your life and allowing it to come in — secondly acknowledging that the source of goodness is outside of yourself. So vocalise your gratitude.

17 STEALING

*"Self-pity is our worst enemy, and if we yield to it, we
can never do anything wise in this world."*
Helen keller

Intriguing subtitle right?....and I am sure you're saying to
yourself that you don't steal or take what isn't yours. You
may feel that your not a thief, but you sneak home a
notebook, a folder, pens or post-it notes from work.
Maybe you don't take physical goods, but you steal
relationships by gossiping and slandering people, maybe at
work, in the community or even about family.

Are you someone who feels they need to step on others
to climb the corporate ladder because someone else has
the job you want, the salary, the perks, the company car,
or network you so desperately want?.

Do you steal peoples energy by always complaining
whenever someone asks you how you are?. Maybe it is
kindness from others you rob by taking it for granted
and not appreciating it. These may sound small issues, and

you may wonder what the problem is, or you may well be aware and know what I mean and choose not to acknowledge it. Either way, you have developed a way of being that says that you don't feel you deserve better and even when you do receive anything good you don't find it easy to accept it and feel grateful. Instead, it is natural for you to take because you get away with doing so because no one says anything to you. You do have a niggardly feeling about it though that you can't shake off about why others have and receive so much.

There are many versions of the old saying "what you give out, you will get back". In essence when you steal and take it for granted, whatever that may be in your life, you are saying that you don't deserve it for yourself and that you are not grateful and don't appreciate what you already have. You therefore have to be sneaky and hide and try to snatch it off others when they are not watching or aware of what you are doing. This all comes from a mind that is unaware and ungrateful of all that you already have.

So if that all sounds like you and you want to do something about it, I applaud you for taking a stand. Write in once you have got to the six-month stage and tell me how it is going, ok. Practically if you find yourself taking from others or even physically stealing items, write it down in the following table. What it is that your taking?. Next write down where it is taken from, for example, if you take stationary from work home, towels, toiletries, bathrobes, slippers, cutlery, coat hangers. Maybe you do none of that but steal from shops or restaurants, regardless of what you take and from where write it down. Then look up the cost of the item(s) be that peoples time, their respect, their dignity or physical objects from the business. Add up the total and then if you could afford to buy those items rather than steal them. If not write down how many weeks it would take to save to buy them. Then do exactly that. I bet my bottom dollar once you have done that you will realise that you did not really want or even need those things you have been stealing.

what you stole?	Where or from whom did you steal?	Cost	Total cost of what you stole	Can you afford it yourself?	Weeks to save to afford it?

Practising gratitude allows the mind to create balance particularly when you are feeling lack and irritation. Focusing on scarcity and the negative aspects of your life will take out the joy from your life, decrease your creativity, create a skewed view of life and your circumstances — besides, both your levels of creativity and empowerment.

It is not about avoiding problems, expecting life to be perfect or dying the truth. Research shows that grateful people are more resistant to stress. Gratitude enables you to see things from a different perspective to allow you to interpret events that could be deemed harmful and thereby provide protection against long term anxiety or trauma. It is evidenced very clearly in Viktor Frankl's 'Man's Search for Meaning'.

Practising gratitude will enable you to participate more in your own life and bring clarity rather than focus on resent and envy and what you don't have as you lean into life. You may find yourself being more generous rather than taking which in turn create further happiness. Gratitude may well often soften your heart if you have shielded it and secured it behind a heavily protected fort from life's knocks and tumbles. Gratitude is an excellent enabler for forgiveness as you meet life with an open heart and letting go of being right and making others wrong. Furthermore, gratitude allows you to be present in your life rather than getting lost or swinging between and identifying and clinging onto one emotion or another. Instead of focusing on what could be, should be, must be, maybe, you can be grateful for what is.

18 WEALTH AND GRATITUDE

"we are not generous until we have given to others what we would have used. Money talks, it says goodbye"?
Brian kluth

We have spoken about the links between gratitude and hoarding, minimalism, stealing, sharing and giving. It is time for a different type of giving. Giving that looks at the relationship between money and gratitude. Just so you are prepared and don't feel I didn't warn you. This chapter may send your internal chatter on at full volume. You may feel like you would instead do 12 rounds in the ring with Tyson, and I wouldn't blame you. It is scary when the words giving and money get mentioned, whether you have a lot or a little.

Every religion encourages people to give from their wealth. The majority of religions tithe. Jews give Maaser; the Muslims give Zakat and the Christians tithe. Tithing aims at helping the person recognise and be grateful to God from whom everything comes. It serves as a reminder that we cannot take it with us at the end of our lives. As a result, agnostics, atheists and many who do not follow a particular religion or sect will generously donate regardless of their beliefs.

Many of the world's wealthiest people and companies tithe regularly. Some say that it is the best route to riches. John D. Rockefeller tithed 10% of his income to his church ever since his first started getting paid. "I would never have been able to tithe the first million dollars I ever made if I had not tithed my first salary, which was $1.50".

Regarded as one of the top investors in the last century, John Templeton stated: "I have observed 100,000 families over my years of investment counselling. I always saw greater prosperity and happiness among those families who tithed than among those who didn't".

Research has shown that giving leads to the path of wealth. Research also highlighted that it has a positive psychological effect on the giver's attitude of how they view wealth. It creates a feeling of wealth when the vast majority of people remain financially unhappy.

Social researcher Arthur C. Brooks looked at the relationship between wealth and giving. He looked at approximately 30,0000 Americans in more than 40 different communities from different backgrounds including financial, education, age, race and religion. His studies revealed that people gave more when they earned more. Furthermore, there is an increase in wealth for people who gave more. The total net impact was not only on the giver and companies but on the nation's economy.

Warren Buffett and Bill Gates have created a Giving Pledge organisation to which they donate more than the normal 10% tithe. They see it as a responsibility to give when they have a lot They requested those who are wealthy donate half of their wealth.

Tithing crosses all boundaries; it serves and benefits everyone regardless of faith. An Irish colleague of mine uses his money to sponsor an orphan in Africa; another colleague purchased goats for families in Africa.

Many celebrities donate, JK Rowling, Prince, George Michael, Elton Jon, England's Footballers Foundation, JJ Watt who plays for the NFL, Houston, Texans. However, many give who are not famous. Chen Shu-Shu sells vegetables in Taiwan. She spends 3 dollars on herself and gives away the rest. She has donated hundreds of thousands of pounds. Her philosophy is that the amount you make is not essential. It is what you do with the money that matters. She stated that anyone could do it. Composer William Corbett said that "thousands upon thousands are yearly brought into a state of real poverty by their great anxiety not to be thought poor". While

Anne Swetchine, a Russian-French Writer said: "We are rich only through what we give, and poor through what we refuse and keep". Chen Shu-Shu herself simply said, "that you cannot take it with you".

You may be wondering what giving money has to do with gratitude?. Perhaps you switched off at the beginning of this chapter?. You may have even skipped the whole section looking for a word or sentence where the focus was back on anything but giving from your wealth. You don't mind, if you have to, donate your time to a few good causes. You may do this once a year at work because the company you work for donate a day or half a day to various local charities. As a result, you go and help, take team photos, which get put into the company magazine. However, the thought of parting with money causes you to have a strange physical reaction. It may just be because you are struggling financially rather than you don't want to give. So you feel rather than sharing a little you would rather not embarrass yourself, and therefore give nothing.

Gratitude, as we have been saying throughout the book, is linked with giving. You allow yourself to come out of your head and focus in the broader community, on the 'we' rather than the 'I'. As Winston Churchill said you create a living by what you receive, but a life out of what you give to others. You give from what you have to help others, and you allow yourself to open up to receive. When you are grateful, you share not out fear or because you have to and don't want to look bad in front of others. Perhaps that is why it is the poor who are the most generous according to a French proverb. Even Anne Frank (Jewish Dutch diarist) highlighted that no one ever became poor by giving. In comparison, American publisher, Malcolm Forbes gets straight to the point "nought, get same. Give much, get same.

When we put gratitude into practice, we feel more grateful and generous. UC (University of California), Berkeley research liken gratitude to a moral barometer whereby one person has benefitted from another's 'moral' actions. Gratitude acts as the cement, or 'moral reinforcement' whereby receiving thanks will lead you to give again. In essence when your grateful your brain becomes more charitable. When you give your brain reinforces the thought that you have something to offer and you become more thankful for what you have.

The Templeton giving survey funded by the John Templeton foundation highlighted that grateful people, people who thought about gratitude daily donated more money and volunteered more hours each year.

Emmons states that gratitude motivates people to 'pay it forward'. It creates a bond between the giver and the receiver. People are left touched moved and inspired to in turn to give more than the good they have received. Generosity and gratitude are closely linked. When you are grateful, you appreciate all the blessings you have and also want to pass them onto others. As a result of one person's generous act, another person is inspired to act in kind. Gratitude allows us to play a more prominent role in all that the world has to offer and make our contribution according to Author William Damon whose research involved surveying more than 1200 people.

You may notice yourself when someone does something for you; you wish to return the favour. The gift of giving and receiving doesn't necessarily stop there. Instead, it isn't even about the person who gave you the gift or helped you.

Through the research on for this book, many people shared how someone had helped them, which inspired them to pay it forward. As a result, they give to others in similar situations echoing the research, and what the Greek Philosopher stated that "true value of money is not in its possession but its use". Inherently grateful people are more empathetic and more likely to share their wealth to help others leaving them touched moved and inspired.

19 BODY GRATEFUL

"Prayers of gratitude are powerful tools for wellness."
Dr Christiane Northrop

Exercise

It does not have to mean pounding the payment every morning at the break of dawn or lifting weights and doing 10k marathons on the treadmill finished off with a leisurely row of 5k on the rowing machine. It could be a simple walk or jog, every morning to get the body morning and the heart pumping. You are grateful for the body and taking care of it because it is taking care of you.

Health

You may have a health condition; it may be a long term health condition such as diabetes or COPD, heart condition, rheumatoid arthritis or any other number of diseases.

Research participants were asked to undertake a simple gratitude practice for three weeks. Robert Emmons assigned participants to the simple task of writing a gratitude journal for three weeks. The research with over one thousand participants aged 8 to 80 who regularly practised gratitude reported multiple benefits.

The research showed as we discussed earlier practising gratitude by keeping a gratitude journal and writing down things that you are grateful for improved sleep and sleep quality so that participants slept longer and felt more refreshed upon waking up. Gratitude journal keepers were reported to have fewer physical symptoms. They spent more time exercising and taking care of their health, had less physical pain, reduced the systolic blood pressure of patients with hypertension, stronger immune systems.

Psychologically the participants reported increased levels of positive emotions, felt higher levels of alertness, aliveness, more awake, increased levels of joy, pleasure, optimism and pleasure.

The participants were also noted to have been affected positively on a social level. They became more helpful, generous and compassionate, levels of forgiveness increased. They became more outgoing and felt less lonely and isolated.

It is clear that as they focused on appreciating what they had in their lives their levels of increased vitality and feelings of appreciation and gratitude helped them to become more relaxed and enjoy their lives. In turn affecting every aspect of their lives as Emmons research highlights. i.e. physical, psychological and social.

Buddhist monk, Thich Nhat Hanh in his book 'How to Love' discusses what love needs to survive. He mentions that one way to nurture our love is to be aware of what we eat. He adds that we tend to think of our "daily nourishment only in terms of what we eat". He states that there are four types of food, i.e. edible, sensory, volition (the motivation and intention that drives us), and consciousness (individual, collective and the environment). In the pages that follow in his book, he explains how important each of these, four types of food are. By moderating and being conscious of what it is that is being consumed, we are showing our body respect and love. On the flip side "whenever we read a magazine we consume, watch TV program we consume. Whatever we consume affects our body and mind. Feeding ourselves with "toxic magazine articles, movies or video games, they will feed our anger and fear" It is through gratitude that you can appreciate your body and take care of it with the respect it deserves. He allows the question to linger, i.e. "perhaps we are afraid to contemplate beauty, and that's why we don't treat our bodies and the bodies of others with respect."

A man who is grateful and is very conscious of what he puts into his body is tennis player, Novak Djokovic, who also came from humble beginnings before rising to fame. He admits his performance is related to taking care of his body and what he eats.

Often we neglect how our body feels and when it changes, we tend to stop caring for it. We forget to be grateful for all the functions it undertakes automatically for us. We complain about everything that is wrong with our body and health rather than what is right, i.e. the good health that we do have. Maybe you don't appreciate your body or fully aware of it because you treat it more as a machine, a tool, however, as the old saying goes, it is the only one you have. Earlier on we discussed the value and taking things for granted. Research shows that positive emotions diminish quickly; however, gratitude enables you to recognise the importance and the advantages and thereby not take it for granted.

Like Emmons confessed and many gratitude advocates we all struggle to be grateful particularly when there some things we need to do, and everything needs our attention as all of us are not trained by the Navy Seals, David Goggins or the Army. I don't know about you, but when there are numerous tasks or jobs to do all at once, and they all need your attention, you end up putting so much pressure on yourself. Then the IT decides not to work, the washing machine determined it won't release the shirt you need for work in the morning. The tumbler dryer smells like its burnt and blows out causing sparks to come out. The fuse blows, sending the whole flat apartment into darkness.

Meanwhile, the boiler packs up and takes a walk and it too you notice is leaking. By now your late for work only to find the battery in your car is dead and you start blaming uncle Jo because you allowed him to fix your car last time. You call work only to find out you have missed your slot in the monthly board meeting so your project cannot be presented and so you cannot be given the funding in this quarter.

All that is going on continuously and you are sure "something's got to give". So sure enough, sooner or later it is your health, and you become ill so that you are left wondering how that arose. However, as Hippocrates stated "illnesses do not come upon us out of the blue. They develop from small daily sins against nature. When enough sins have accumulated illnesses will suddenly appear".

Practising gratitude for the health, you have maybe the simplest of resolves to start. Start with the gratitude journal noting down all the things that your body does and has done so far for you. Start there. Exactly where you are. Moreover, be grateful.

THANKS

Thanks for reading 'Gratitude and You' and thank you to everyone who has already replied. If this book has made an impact on you, I would love to hear about it. Ping me an email at gratitudeandyou@outlook.com

If you would like to continue your growth and development and improve the results in all the different areas of your life, please consider joining me for one to one training or bringing me into your organisation.

Printed in Great Britain
by Amazon